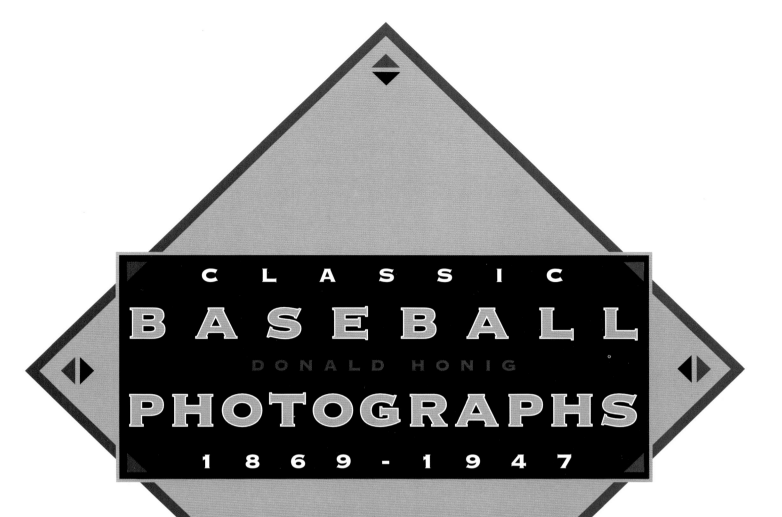

CLASSIC
BASEBALL
DONALD HONIG
PHOTOGRAPHS
1869 - 1947

CLASSIC
BASEBALL
DONALD HONIG
PHOTOGRAPHS
1869 - 1947

SMITHMARK

This edition published in 1999 by SMITHMARK Publishers,
a division of U.S. Media Holdings, Inc.,
115 West 18th Street, New York, NY 10011.

SMITHMARK books are available for bulk purchase for sales promotion and premium use. For details write
or call the manager of special sales, SMITHMARK Publishers, 115 West 18th Street, New York, NY 10011.

ISBN 0-7651-1055-5

Printed in Hong Kong

10 9 8 7 6 5 4 3 2 1

Library of Congress Cataloging-in-Publication Data

Honig, Donald.
    [Shadows of summer]
    Classic baseball photographs, 1869-1947 / Donald Honig.
        p.   cm.
    Previously published: Shadows of summer. New York : Viking Studio
    Books, 1994.
    Incldes index.
    ISBN 0-7651-1055-5 (alk. paper)
    1. Baseball--United States--History--19th century.   2. Baseball-
    -United States--History--20th century.   3. Baseball--United States-
    -Pictorial works.   I. Title.
    [GV863.A1H656   1999]
    796.357'0973--dc21   98-47866
                                                                  CIP

Contents

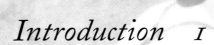

Foreword

A remarkable thing happened the morning after I was asked to write this foreword to Donald Honig's landmark book. At least, I think it was remarkable, considering the coincidence. I was walking from my house to a store a quarter of a mile away. I went past a church, through a schoolyard, and along a fence bounding the school playground. There in the grass outside the fence was a baseball.

It wasn't brand new but it was new enough, a good ball, white and gleaming in the grass. It was early in the morning, and no one was in the playground or near it. No one was there, and the ball was sitting up in the grass like a freshly sprouted mushroom. So I plucked it. I picked it up and looked around. Nobody. The ball was mine. As a kid would say belligerently, I found it.

I walked onto a road, tossing the ball in one hand, not at all concerned about the possible reaction of people driving by (what's that old guy doing with a baseball?). I kept moving the ball with my fingers, spinning it, gripping the seams, occasionally tossing it back and forth from one hand to the other. It was a wonderful, satisfying feeling. I found myself thinking of a line in Philip Larkin's great poem "Church Going," in which, not at all religious, he nonetheless stops to enter an empty church in the English countryside. "It pleases me to stand in silence here," Larkin wrote, and it pleased me that silent Saturday morning to feel a baseball in my hand as I walked to the store.

I think my pleasure in the baseball echoes the pleasure to be derived from the splendid old photographs in this book, to which Don Honig has written such a perfect accompaniment in text and captions. It's part nostalgia, of course. I couldn't throw a baseball today from home plate to second base, but handling the ball brought back the essence of the days when I could. Nostalgia is in these photographs, too, even though many of them are from a time that even people my age are too young to remember.

But it's more than nostalgia. The naked baseball sitting in the grass that morning was simple, hard, honest, and, in a way, defiant. This is all I am, it seemed to say. Just a baseball. From a game that kids play here. No glitz, no luxury boxes, no state-of-the-art scoreboards, no p.a. systems, no TV commercials. Baseball. Nothing more.

The photographs here have the same impact. Like the baseball they are simple, direct, and uncompromising. Not everything was good in the good old days, and the photos show the rough fields, the rickety grandstands, the bulky, wrinkled uniforms, and, yes, the lack of black players in organized baseball. The book depicts Satchel Paige, Josh Gibson, and other superb players in the old Negro Leagues, but, significantly, it ends in 1947, the year Jackie Robinson broke the color barrier and baseball entered a new era. The warm portrait of the young, smiling Robinson with Pee Wee Reese and the other members of the Brooklyn infield on Opening Day that historic year accents the unalterable truth that there were almost no black faces in organized baseball before Jackie came along.

I say "almost" because Honig includes a marvelous picture of Kid Elberfeld, an ex–major leaguer who managed in the minors in the early decades of the century, sitting at the edge of a dugout bantering with two young black Americans sitting with him. Their names were Archie and Red, and Elberfeld used them in those days of small squads and all but nonexistent coaching staffs to warm up his pitchers. They are not in uniform but one has a catcher's mitt and is holding a baseball. "Elberfeld's pair of irregulars," Honig writes, "were good enough for the skipper to take them on road trips with the club." In the photo there is an ease and affection and shared pleasure among the three that is palpable. It makes one realize almost achingly that even in that whites-only era baseball was the black man's game too, and that he was at home in it, as Paige, Gibson, and the others had already demonstrated, and as Robinson and so many others proved triumphantly in the major leagues from 1947 on.

But this book is not a treatise on sociology. It's an archaeological dig, a peek into the distant past, and it says, "This is what it was like." John McGraw lolling against a fence chatting with Honus Wagner. Three St. Louis Cardinals outfielders posing for the camera in the 1920s in knicker-length uniforms and knee-length uniform stockings. Three Philadelphia Athletics outfielders from the same era, dressed the same way, posing the same way. Rube Waddell, wearing a warmup jacket with enormous buttons, his face suspicious or perhaps defiant, his body tilted slightly to one side (which suited his off-center personality), standing in front of an old scoreboard on which only parts of team names can be seen: HICAGO, LEVELAN, ETROI. Three more Cardinals, these from the hard-bitten Gashouse Gang of the 1930s, standing, sitting, crouching at the edge of the dugout, appraising with tough, expressionless faces something on the field and looking as though they knew what they would do about it.

Many of the early pictures are posed, but are nonetheless acutely natural and refreshing, with the players, who were not at all that used to cameras, looking at the lens (and therefore at us) with curiosity, reluctance, amusement, even eagerness (like kids of that era saying, "Take my picture!" whenever they saw someone with a camera). Posed or not, almost all the photographs are arresting. Note the one of writer Ring Lardner and actor George M. Cohan in the Chicago Cubs dugout with Manager Joe McCarthy—the tense Lardner staring at the camera with his hard straw hat off, the relaxed Cohan smiling at it with his hard straw hat on.

Several of the photographs are works of art. The Gashouse Gang picture mentioned above is a masterpiece of composition. A simple shot of Jack Coombs in the locker room, putting on his spikes, has lighting Caravaggio would have killed for. A portrait of Pete Gray, the wartime St. Louis Browns' one-armed outfielder, posing on the ballfield with his slender father

and his massive mother, is Americana beyond Grant Wood.

There are the classic photos: Ty Cobb exploding into third base; graceful Joe DiMaggio in full swing; aging Honus Wagner contemplating a bat; hatless Christy Mathewson throwing right at you. There are revealing, informative pictures: Miller Huggins choking up almost a foot on his bat; Zack Wheat showing concentrated power that shouts, "This was a hitter!"; Mike Gonzales in a wiry lopsided catcher's mask that makes you wonder how catchers survived in those good old days.

And there are the faces, unforgettable faces: Walter Johnson with the brim of his cap lowered over his eyes; Grover Cleveland Alexander, his visage strong and sad; a young, remarkably handsome Casey Stengel; the boyish Pete Reiser, Brooklyn's darling in 1941; Bill Carrigan, Babe Ruth's first big league manager, whose nickname was "Rough," and when you see his picture you know why; Cobb again, with his piercing eyes and sneering mouth; Gil Hodges, before he was a first baseman, in catcher's gear with his cap on backwards but intensely serious; Ted Williams before World War II, when he was still "the kid" with a goofy grin.

There is a reality, a naturalness, a closeness evinced in these pictures. The men portrayed may be gods in a baseball sense, but they're people, too, ordinary people, closer to the fans and the fans' way of life than the wildly wealthy, extravagantly publicized players of today can ever hope to be. Baseball in the old days was something like a hand saw and a hammer compared to today's power saw and electric nail-driver. Not superior—a power saw and a nail-driver will do most jobs faster and better—but maybe prettier to contemplate. It's the way things used to be, and it's a nice feeling using a hand saw and a hammer now and then. Brings back memories.

In short, beauty is in the eye of the beholder. This is a beautiful book, as beautiful as the baseball in the grass.

—Robert W. Creamer

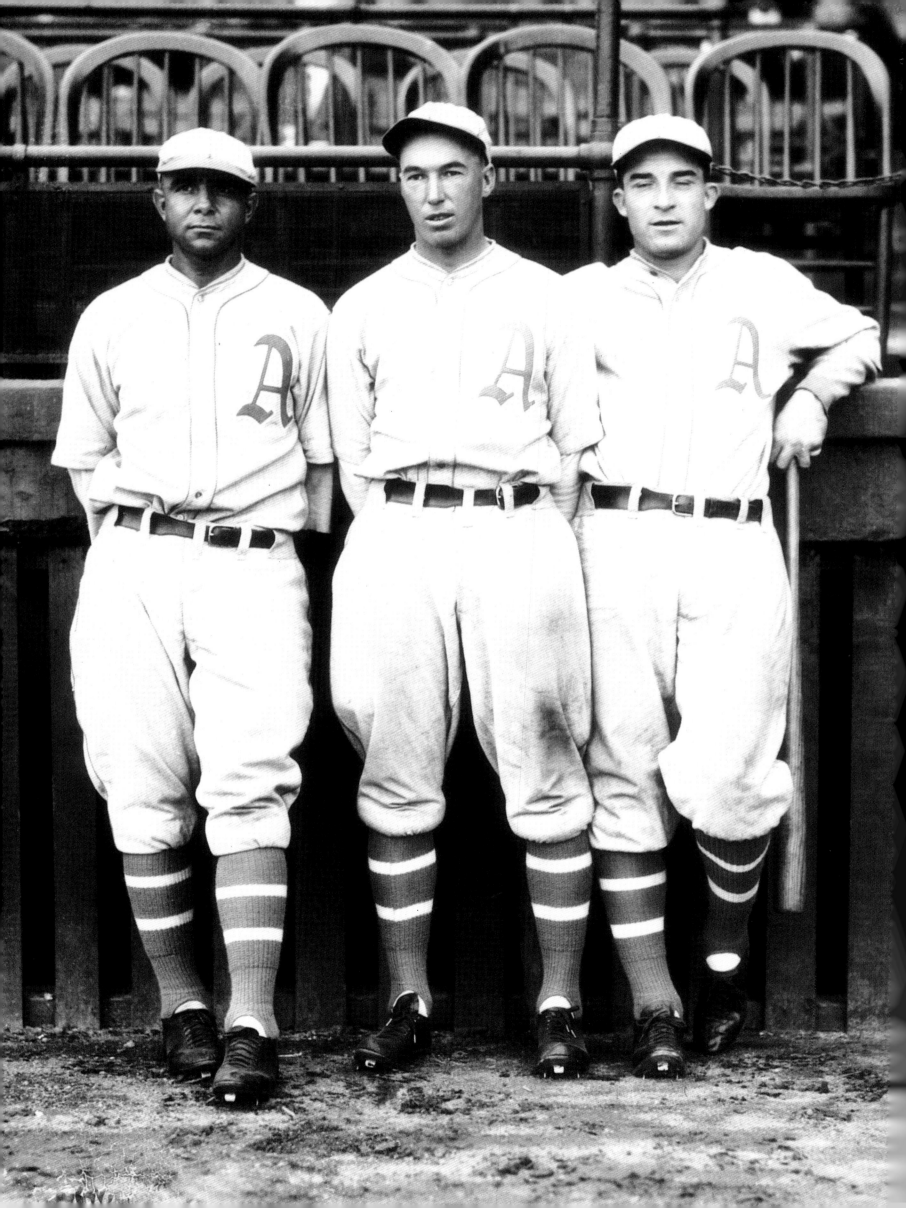

Introduction

Facing page: Evidently uninterested and impatient for the camera to record them for future stargazers are the regular outfielders on Connie Mack's 1929–31 pennant-winning Philadelphia Athletics. They are, from left to right, **BING MILLER, MULE HAAS,** and **AL SIMMONS.** The picture was taken at Philadelphia's Shibe Park, where the expensive seats appear more suitable to a courtroom than a ballpark.

Pages 2 & 3: These gentlemen, the **1869 CINCINNATI RED STOCKINGS,** represent the first professional baseball team ever to take the field. This ten-man squad traveled the country from New York to San Francisco, taking on all comers and returning home with a 57–0 record. The interest the team stimulated in baseball helped lead in 1871 to the formation of the National Association of Professional Baseball Players, which was organized baseball's shaky embryo. Its five-year existence of trial and error led to the founding of the National League in 1876. With that, baseball was on its way.

No game has been as diligently and lovingly chronicled as baseball. From its inception in the 1840s, the game has been statistically inscribed, at bat by at bat. Newspapers and then "official" guides recorded those numbers, thereby imbuing the game with a history.

Fleshing out the numbers are the stories and the people. No other sport has delivered up the characters and the personalities that baseball has. Thanks to the length of its season and the leisurely pace of its performance, there is time for stories to develop, be told, and indeed be passed along from one generation to the next. Anecdotes attributed to Dizzy Dean are found to have originated with Rube Wad-

At New York's Hilltop Park in 1910, right-hander TOM HUGHES loosens up alongside outfielder Harry Wolter.

Hughes pitched for the Yankees in 1909 and 1910 with moderate success. Tom's glory moment came on June 16, 1916, when as a Boston Brave he no-hit the Pittsburgh Pirates, 2–0, ending with a flourish when he fanned Honus Wagner for the final out.

Once upon a time a deaf-mute athlete could be nicknamed "Dummy" without protest from anyone. That was what they called right-handed pitcher LUTHER HADEN TAYLOR, *opposite*, who played from 1900 to 1908, mostly with the New York Giants. His best year was 1904, when he won 22 games, only to be overshadowed by a pair of 30-game-winning team-mates, Christy Mathewson and "Iron Man" Joe McGinnity.

dell, and while some of that diligent research may prove that tales spun about such mountaintop figures as Babe Ruth or Honus Wagner may be somewhat less than true, those stories continue to be told and believed because they are too good not to be true. Anyway, they "feel" right, which is good enough for the lifelong fan, because what the imagination has chosen to caress it will not discard.

The game's mighty compendium of statistics is an essential part of the baseball fan's romantic liaison with his game. Those numbers, indelibly part of the memory bank, are not merely numbers but also quasi-genetic realities from which athletes take form, veritable DNAs of speed, power, and endurance.

From the turn of the century on, the numbers were accompanied increasingly by faces and thus given further dimension, for now there was another constant at the ballpark—the photographer. These men, in the beginning most notably Charles M. Conlon and Paul Thompson, who worked for New York City newspapers, carried their cumbersome cameras and glass negatives out to the ballparks and began the work of photographing virtually every player, home team and visitor alike.

Most nineteenth-century ballplayers had their pictures taken in photographers' studios, where they donned their uniforms, stood before an ingenuously painted mural that was supposed to depict a ballpark, and struck a pose, sometimes holding a bat, sometimes reaching for a baseball suspended in midair from a just-visible wire, sometimes even sprawling across the floor to simulate a slide. Maybe it was the formality of the studio setting, but many of the players have affected, ceremonious poses, their faces sober and unsmiling.

It isn't until after the turn of the century, when players began to be photographed in their natural element of sunshine, grass, grandstands, and baseball noises, that serenity begins to appear in their faces, that solemn expressions are replaced by an athlete's pride and vigor. There is now the relaxed informality that conveys the at-home equanimity of a man utterly comfortable where he stands.

Baseball is probably at its most faultlessly enchanting during pregame workouts, when its finest practitioners are able to engage in it with the same pure zest with which they first discovered it. There is no pressure, no tension, merely the unalloyed full-bodied exhilaration that lies at the game's very core. There is a primal joy in embryonic abilities re-creating once again what impelled them as children and has now set them among a select handful who can do what millions of their countrymen can only cherish and envy. Then and now, that spirit is captured by the photographers who wander about the field during these workouts.

It seems historically correct for on-field, sunshine photography to have become a permanent part of baseball at the turn of the century, for it was then that the game's "modern" era began rocking in its cradle. Just a few years before, the pitcher had been moved from fifty feet away from home plate to sixty feet, six inches (the six inches coming from an early, never-corrected mismeasurement), joining the geometrically perfect ninety feet between bases as a consummate baseball standard. With the formation of the American League in 1901, major league baseball settled into its two-league structure, with the World Series following in 1903 to shape the season's natural culmination.

Before the years of rapid communication, the big leagues' rela-

They march in lockstep through the first two decades of the century: Mathewson, Johnson, and **GROVER CLEVELAND ALEXANDER,** *opposite,* inseparable by pitching might and the legends of their achievements.

Seen here as a rookie in 1911, Alexander set the still-standing record for first-year pitchers with 28 victories. Greater heights awaited— three consecutive 30-victory seasons from 1915–17.

Alex retired in 1930 with a lifetime victory total of 373, leaving him in a tie for the National League lead with the only man who had ever been a match for him—Mathewson. It remains one of the most intriguing and most felicitously calibrated statistical deadlocks in baseball history.

Pages 8 & 9: That white blur under **DODE PASKERT'S** right sleeve tells us that the Cincinnati outfielder has just swung through a batting practice delivery. The picture was taken in 1909, the first of three years that the Reds wore these dark blue road uniforms.

Paskert was one of those players of whom it can truly be said that they form the backbone of the game. Never stars, they are like infantry regulars, performing with fidelity and consistency, then departing in anonymity, leaving behind them barely a spike mark to notch their passage. (For his 1907–1921 career Paskert averaged .268.)

Perhaps typically, Paskert's finest moment occurred away from the roar of the crowd when, in 1920, he helped save 15 children from a burning apartment building in his native Cleveland.

tionship with many of its fans might be described as being of remote intimacy, particularly with those fans who lived in rural areas of the country, as so many did in the century's opening decades. Ernie Shore, who a few years later was pitching for the Boston Red Sox, recalled "all the excitement" of the 1910 World Series in his small North Carolina town, and how that excitement had to remain in suspension because "in those days you had to wait until the next day to get the score. You just stayed on the edge until you finally got hold of that newspaper. I can remember one of the fellows taking out his pocket watch one afternoon and looking at it and saying, 'Well, they're started. The game's on.' That was about as close as you got to it in those days—knowing when the game was on and trying to imagine what was happening."

Despite its general popularity, for decades baseball was hardly looked upon as a profession for respectable young men. Gentlemen icons like Christy Mathewson, Walter Johnson, and Honus Wagner to the contrary, ballplayers had a reputation as drunkards and carousers, and indeed club rosters included a number of free spirits. Where today first-class hotels vie for the patronage of big league clubs, in the early years of the century these particular travelers were not welcome at the better establishments.

If the welcome mat was often snatched away at the approach of a squad of big leaguers, it was sometimes not without reason. A tale is told of a half-dozen Detroit Tigers, circa 1908, who once gathered in the corridor of their hotel for an impromptu game of craps. Alerted by the seductive clicking of the cubes, catcher Charlie Schmidt was roused from his slumber, rose from his bed, and in his white, ankle-length nightshirt

Was managing a tougher job in the old days? Well, the skipper's job description certainly called for more diversification. For one thing, clubs generally carried only one coach, if even that. This picture, taken at New York's Polo Grounds in 1910, depicts Dodger manager **BILL DAHLEN**, comfortably buttoned up in his warmup sweater, slamming the ball around the infield, a chore no big league manager would dream of handling today.

The man ready to take the pegs behind Bill is catcher Bill Bergen, statistically big league baseball's most anemic hitter. Playing in 947 games from 1901 to 1911, he came to bat 3,028 times, managing just 516 hits, for a lifetime average of .170. It is safe to assume that Bill was one hell of a defensive catcher.

(then de rigueur bedtime apparel) left his room and, money in hand, squatted down to join his mates at their game of chance. But the dice were unkind to Charlie and his money was soon in other hands. The disgruntled Charlie watched the game for a few more minutes, then rose and returned to his room—leaving behind a neat pile of turds to mark his place.

There were other tales of pliant women smuggled into hotels via side doors or hoisted in and out of windows, of irate athletes invading the kitchen to avenge overcooked steaks, of players demonstrating sliding techniques across polished lobby floors. Hardly genteel behavior, but these were not for the most part genteel young men. But social pariahs or not, to a large segment of the country they were heroes.

Baseball's growth and development is evident throughout this gallery of photographs, each selected for its evocation of a man and a time and a place. The ongoing passage of time is marked by the changes in uniform styles, equipment (or non-equipment: note the catchers of the century's first decade playing without shinguards), and the dress of spectators, whose derbies and straw boaters and black suits and starched collars make their fashion statements and then disappear. Playing surfaces now receive more expert care, and huge concrete and steel structures have replaced combustible wooden grandstands. In the 1930s towers of electric light bulbs begin appearing on grandstand roofs, creating a new era as well as a new aura for the old game of sunlight and shadows.

There is another change, a human one. Faces, particularly of the early years—compare them with those of today. Today's faces radiate with the strength and pride of bracing health. They seem younger than their same-age counterparts of yesteryear, more resistant to time. The young men of generations gone rose from a harder, more laboring world. Without the benefit of modern diets, health care, physical conditioning, more solicitous attention to injuries, they appear older than their years, their prematurely lined faces and tobacco-stained smiles manifesting a tougher and poorer road to success, a less compromising deal with their profession.

"He was the most wonderful individual it was ever my privilege to know. It was an honor to be his friend and teammate."

The "he" that EDDIE AINSMITH refers to was his old Washington Senators batterymate Walter Johnson, whose swifties Eddie caught from 1910 through 1918. The pitcher also had high praise for his catching. "I am always comfortable pitching to Eddie Ainsmith," said Walter, always quick with a testimonial.

Here we find Eddie returning a pregame warmup toss. To Walter, perhaps?

Baseball was no less a business then than it is today, minus the millions of dollars and the agents and the lawyers and the Major League Players Association, though the seeds of the latter were surely being planted back then. Salary arbitration was unknown, and if a player held out too stubbornly for more money, he was informed that the club would simply get along without him. Callousness toward pain was commonplace; unless he had a truly disabling injury, a man was expected to play. In the spring of 1913, when Smoky Joe Wood, a thirty-four-game-winning right-hander for the Red Sox in 1912, injured his arm, the club rushed him back to action prematurely and ruined the twenty-three-year-old wonder pitcher forever. Imagine a thirty-game winner today (if one ever did wander back into captivity): At the merest twinge he would be put on the disabled list and vigilantly submitted to all that modern medical science could afford. A different world indeed.

Another reflection of the times is the absence, until after World War II, of black players in the major leagues, victims of society's bland acceptance of racial discrimination and of baseball's unwritten law of exclusion. Because it was never formally enacted, this unwritten law was a near-unbreakable piece of legislation, and thus America's game existed as a citadel of institutionalized hypocrisy. Even as its chroniclers idealized the game as the perfect national pastime, its reigning moguls and cheerleaders chose to ignore its nondemocratic guidelines. Ty Cobb was no hypocrite: Giving expression to a raw cultural integrity, the game's premier player (until the arrival of Babe Ruth, who had no such propensities) stated that he would not step on the same field with a black. Even Connie Mack, baseball's purest figure of secular veneration, was adamant about maintaining the color barrier. John McGraw, however,

with his insatiable appreciation for talent, tried to finesse the issue by slipping a black player onto the team in the guise of an American Indian. But somebody blew the whistle and even the autocratic Mr. McGraw had to yield to the invisible barrier. It wasn't until 1947 (when this volume concludes) that big league baseball finally saw its first black player take the field—Jackie Robinson, with the Brooklyn Dodgers.

Any significant modification has always taken place inside the game's essential contours. The lively ball—introduced with acute timeliness for the freewheeling 1920s—the farm system, night ball, the end of the color barrier, artificial playing surfaces, free agency, the domed stadium—all were responses to a changing world, a world the insular game joined only when suitable or necessary.

Otherwise it remains in perpetual renewal, this game of men and numbers, of myths and legends. It is at one with the seasons, leaping to life with springtime, stretching its long, seductive legs through the languorous months of summer, culminating its marathon run with the fall of the leaves and the end of climatic tranquility.

It is the clockless game, the only one not beholden to time. Within its combinations it has formed its own singular universe. Its mystique assures the continuing flow of its lifeblood—those gifted young athletes who never cease to appear on sandlots, in spring camps, in Opening Day lineups, their dreams as changeless as the game they yearn to play. Look into their faces and know that as dreamers they all began equal, star and journeyman alike. It is in the fulfillment of those dreams that the camera has found them and sent them on into time. See them when days were old and they were young, when the moment was fresh, when youth seemed without end and the sunlight forever.

Page 17: Top row, left to right: **ZACK WHEAT,** the long-ago toast of Brooklyn baseball. **RED DOOIN,** turn of the century Phillies catcher. **PATSY DOUGHERTY,** who hit the National League's first home run in World Series competition (1903). *Center row, left to right:* **PATSY DONOVAN,** big league outfielder from 1890 to 1907. **EWELL ("REB") RUSSELL,** Chicago White Sox left-hander. **FERDIE SCHUPP,** a 21-game winner for the Giants in 1917. *Bottom row, left to right:* **DANNY HOFFMAN,** big league outfielder from 1903–1911. **BOBBY WALLACE.** At one time they called him "Mr. Shortstop." But then along came Wagner. **JOHN ("DOTS") MILLER,** World War I–era infielder.

An array of New York Yankees loosening up in spring training. The Yankees wore their famous pinstripes for the first time in 1912, but didn't adopt them permanently until 1915.

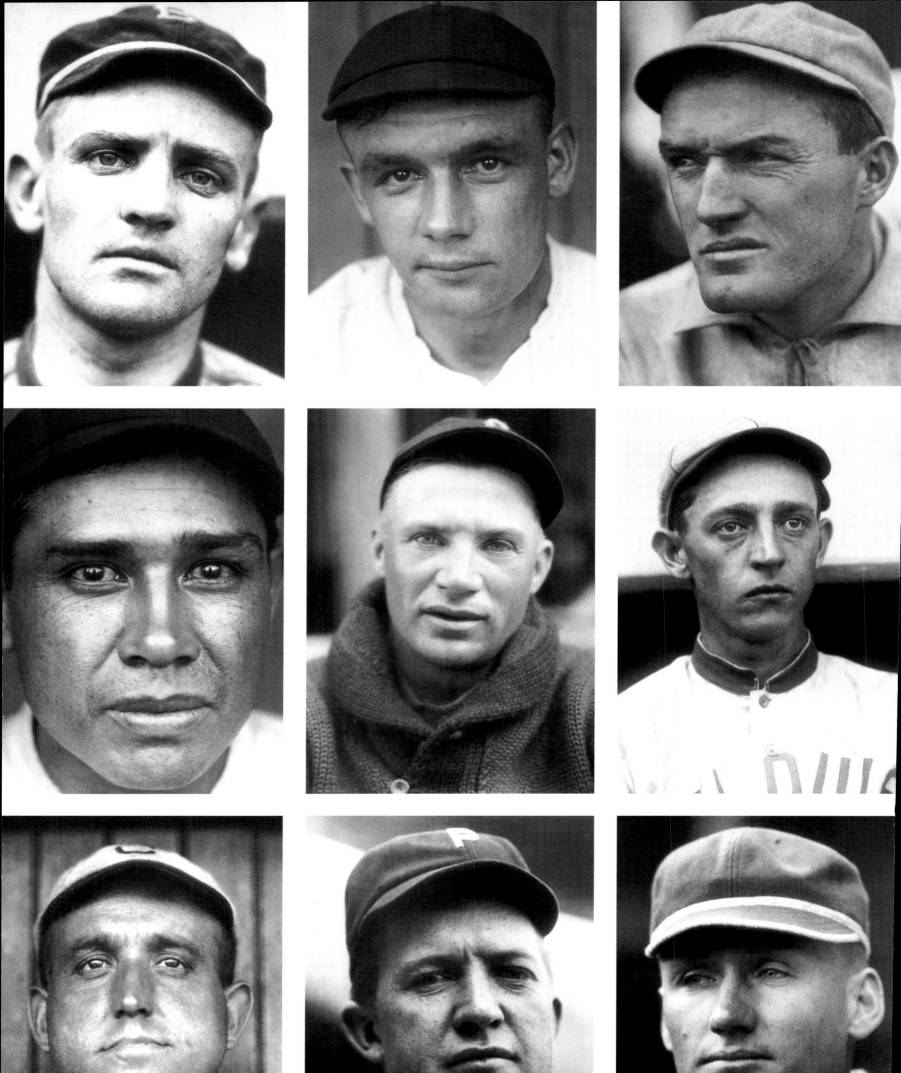

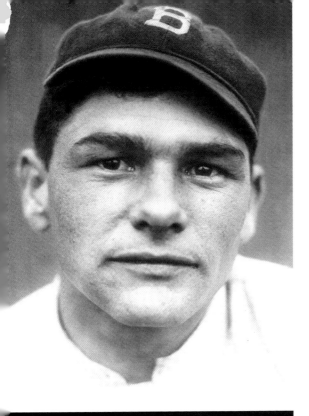

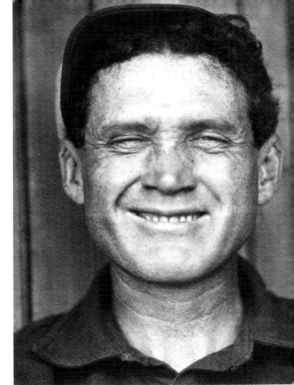

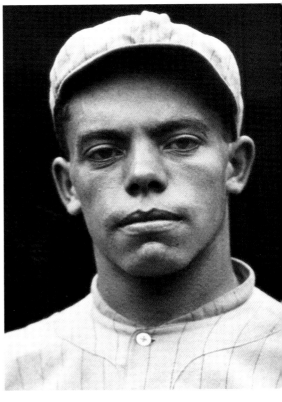

1900–1919

He was eccentric, unreliable, exasperating, and a manager's headache, but GEORGE EDWARD ("RUBE") WADDELL was one thunderous pitcher. The hierarchy of left-handers begins with Rube: Waddell, Grove, Hubbell, Spahn, Koufax, Carlton. None were better than Connie Mack's ace.

Waddell legends abound. He would disappear for a few days to go fishing (during the season), he would go racing at the sound of a passing fire engine (during a game); he loved whiskey, ice cream, red ties, and marriage, committing to the latter at least four times. When he was winning—almost 100 games for the Athletics between 1902 and 1905—all was tolerated, but when Rube's fastball began to cool, so did the tolerance.

Mack traded him to the Browns in 1908, and two years later Rube was gone from the majors. In 1914, at age thirty-seven, he died of tuberculosis.

Decades later a reminiscing Mack said of his wayward, long-gone ace, "He gave me fits. But that fellow could pitch. He could really pitch."

The timing was almost liturgically perfect: a new century and a new major league, in simultaneous birth. Since its formation in 1876, the National League had been professional baseball's dominant force. Upstart competitors like the American Association, the Union Association, and the Players' League had come and gone. After the 1899 season, the National League, operating under an unwieldy twelve-team structure, trimmed four teams from the roster and reorganized itself into a tidier eight-team federation.

It was at this point that Byron Bancroft Johnson, the steel-willed and autocratic president of the Western Association, strongest of the minor leagues,

St. Louis Cardinals first baseman **JAKE BECKLEY** taking
five during workouts before a
game in 1905. In Jake's day,
teams didn't carry more than
seventeen or eighteen players,
so a bit of respite was always
welcome. At this moment the
old warrior was two years away
from the end of his twenty-
year big league career. Perhaps
he is wondering where it has
all gone.

Jake, whose shade made
it to the Hall of Fame in 1971,
seems to have had an exuber-
ant side; when his bat was
smoking (as it often did for a
man with a .308 lifetime average), he was known to shout
out "Chickazoola" as he
watched his base hits drop in.

Opposite: **BAN JOHNSON**
founded the American
League, which he ran with an
iron fist until ill health forced
his resignation in 1927.

made his long-planned move. Shedding his circuit's regional character,
Johnson expanded. With entrepreneurial daring, he established franchises in the National League–abandoned cities of Washington, Cleveland, and Baltimore, made two-team cities of Boston, Chicago, and
Philadelphia, set up shop in Milwaukee and Detroit, rechristened his
confection the American League, and declared it a major league.

The National League, until now a smug, monopolistic, high-
handed operation (with a $2,400 salary cap among its provocations),
suddenly found itself in open warfare. The prizes in this combat were
baseball's sole commodity—players. With well-heeled owners running
his franchises, Johnson encouraged them to flap their checkbooks. The
sound was seductive and National League stalwarts began responding.
Stars like Cy Young, Nap Lajoie, Ed Delahanty, Sam Crawford, Wee
Willie Keeler, Bobby Wallace, Jesse Burkett, Jimmy Collins, and others
began sudden migrations to the new, dollar-green pastures.

Given credibility by these star players, the American League was
an immediate success, by its second season (1902) outdrawing its older
rival in total attendance. A year later the National League, after much
posturing and some expensive litigation, finally accepted the newcomers

as a permanent fixture and by mutual agreement put an end to the ruinous raids on each other's rosters. Cementing the accord was a plan to have the respective league champions meet in a postseason series to determine a "world champion." Thus, up from the fading smoke of interleague warfare came that unique American institution, the World Series, which remains today sport's most sumptuous banquet.

From 1901 through 1919 the big leagues entertained their customers in what has become known as the dead-ball era, playing its games with a lifeless, smudged, sometimes misshapen ball. Home run leaders seldom reached double digits, and many of the circuit shots were inside-the-park efforts. The real "long ball" of the time was the triple, with batters hitting four or five times as many of them as they did home runs.

It was the era of the bunt, the sacrifice, the stolen base. The premier exponent of this style of offense was Detroit's Tyrus Raymond Cobb, who entered the American League as an eighteen-year-old outfielder in 1905; by the time he left in 1928 the record book read like a compilation of "Ty Cobb and others." In 1907, Cobb began a run of twelve batting championships in thirteen years, an unprecedented and still unequaled reign during which he averaged .378.

The era turned out some of baseball's foundation names, men who set records and standards that became touchstones for future icons to be measured against: Cobb, Honus Wagner, Walter Johnson, Eddie Collins, Rube Waddell, Tris Speaker, Nap Lajoie, Shoeless Joe Jackson, Mordecai "Three Finger" Brown, Christy Mathewson, Grover Cleveland Alexander. Remarkable players all, with some among them possessing dimensions enough to slip them into national folklore.

Tilting the game even further in favor of the pitchers during the dead-ball days was the legality of the spitball and other doctored deliveries, in addition to scuffed and torn balls being allowed to remain in play. This latter fact probably accounts for a bit of text from the Walter Johnson legend, namely that Walter threw so hard that you could actually hear the ball go past you. Well, with a bit of torn cover flapping freely, that was entirely possible.

Things changed somewhat in 1910, when the club owners, feeling that the low-scoring games were beginning to have a soporific effect on

the fans, gave the ball a slight injection of animation. They achieved this by introducing a cork center, covered with an eighth of an inch of rubber. The change was immediately apparent, with home run totals more than doubling and league batting averages taking a leap upward.

Baseball then went on to survive two wars, one internal, the other external. The first erupted in 1914 when the minor Federal League declared itself a major league and went into competition with the two established circuits, which suddenly found themselves reliving a past scenario as the Federal League began trying to lure players with higher-paying contracts. Outside of a few fading names like Three Finger Brown and Eddie Plank, however, most of the well-known players stayed put (with salary increases helping define the loyalties of some players). After two indifferent seasons, the Federal League collapsed.

World War I had begun in Europe in 1914 and by the spring of 1917 America was in it. While many major leaguers were called to mil-

There were those who thought **MIKE DONLIN** had what it took to be one of baseball's elite players around the turn of the century, if only he had taken the game more seriously. But the roar of the baseball crowd wasn't enough for "Turkey Mike"—so called for his strut—who found the roar beyond the footlights equally enchanting.

Here Mike is receiving a gold bat in a 1911 Polo Grounds ceremony and giving the camera his best stage-struck grin. On the left are outfielder George Burns, pitcher Hooks Wiltse, and Mathewson, who is admiring the flag-decorated box that held Donlin's bat.

GEORGE SISLER probably came as close to ballplaying perfection as any man who ever wore spikes. The St. Louis Browns first baseman not only did beyond full measure what a player is supposed to do, but like Joe DiMaggio, did it with a flawless artistry.

Like his mighty contemporary, Babe Ruth, Sisler entered the American League as a left-handed pitcher in 1915, but his crackling line-drive bat soon put an end to his mound career. He batted .407 in 1920 and .420 in 1922. An attack of influenza that winter led to a sinus infection that brought on a case of double vision that forced him to sit out the 1923 season. He was never the same thereafter.

After the 1925 season George lamented his decline. He had batted .345 and collected 224 hits. "That wasn't hitting," he said sadly.

itary service and others left the game to enter war-related industries (the provost marshal had issued a "work or fight" edict), unlike during World War II, few players suffered extended career interruptions.

Baseball underwent its severest crisis when the story broke that seven Chicago White Sox players had conspired to throw the 1919 World Series to the Cincinnati Reds (an eighth player was implicated for having been aware of the scheme and not reporting it). When the scandal became public at the end of the 1920 season, many of the game's insiders were unsurprised. Gambling had long been a festering, tacitly accepted part of the diamond scene. For years players had been known to bet on games, the most notorious offender being first baseman Hal Chase, already traded several times for these proclivities. A superlative defensive player, Chase sometimes bet against his own team, then went out on the field and protected his investment with some skillful missteps.

Concerned about public disillusionment, the club owners hired a commissioner and conferred upon him tsarlike powers. A federal judge, Kenesaw Mountain Landis was the right man at the right time. The unforgiving, autocratic Landis promptly rid professional baseball of the offending White Sox players and others implicated in gambling schemes, giving baseball the restorative surge of integrity it so badly needed.

In 1909 Brooklyn Dodgers owner Charles Ebbets, in an address at the club owners' winter meeting, made the statement that "baseball is in its infancy." The statement was prophetic. The game was indeed still in infancy, and fittingly it was a Babe who was about to lead it to thunderous maturity.

They never spoke of **NAPOLEON LAJOIE** without using the word "graceful" to describe him at work. A second baseman for the Philadelphia Phillies from 1896 to 1900, he jumped to the American League in 1901 and promptly set its all-time mark for batting with a .422 average.

Nap spent his banner years with the Cleveland Indians, whom he managed from 1905–1909. He attained such popularity that during his years as skipper the team was known as "the Naps."

Once upon a time the quiet, self-effacing Frenchman was first choice as all-time second baseman, but he was later displaced by Eddie Collins and Rogers Hornsby. But never doubt how highly the witnesses of the past regarded Lajoie. In 1936, when the Hall of Fame was established, the first five inductees were those building blocks of modern baseball, Ty Cobb, Babe Ruth, Christy Mathewson, Honus Wagner, and Walter Johnson. When the electors made their next selection a year later, the name was Lajoie.

Facing Page: Sitting meditatively, collar sleekly raised, **OTTO HESS** awaits the camera to complete the theft of a moment from time. Born in Berne, Switzerland, in 1878, Hess came from the shadows of the Bernese Alps to the New World, where he became one of baseball's prized possessions—a 20-game winner. The slim left-hander notched exactly that number of victories for the 1906 Cleveland Indians, whose uniform he wears with such quiet dignity. It was his only truly successful season on the diamonds of his adopted land.

Otto was one of many baseball talents whose families arrived in America with the immigrant waves of the nineteenth century, most of them Irish, but some from Germany, England, and other lands. Whereas certain areas of commerce looked upon the newcomers with jaundiced eyes, baseball, with its insatiable needs for talented youngsters, was democracy swung wide—as long as you were white.

Pages 30 & 31: It is Hot Springs, Arkansas, the year 1907, and the New York Yankees are at spring training. This neatly upholstered group has come together on the porch of their hotel to allow recording of the occasion. The coats, turtlenecks, and array of hats tell us it was probably not one of Hot Springs' balmier days.

The group contains some notable baseball names. The front row includes, left to right, after the unidentified gentleman at far left, catcher Lou Kleinow, shortstop Bill Dahlen (with the Giants and probably visiting), shortstop Kid Elberfeld, pitcher Bill Hogg (who died two years later at the age of twenty-nine), unidentified, and pitcher Jack Chesbro, a 41-game winner in 1904. Standing above Chesbro is Wee Willie Keeler, next to him is manager Clark Griffith, while the thoughtful young man next to Griff is none other than Branch Rickey, an erudite but weak-hitting catcher. Next to Rickey is Sam Crane, a well-known sportswriter of the day. The elderly gentleman next to Crane is not identified, but next to him is first baseman Jake Stahl. The other men are not identified. Outside of Keeler's wry look they are an impassive group. Maybe they knew they were going to finish fifth that year.

Hot Springs was the site of big league ball's first spring training camp, when Cap Anson brought his Chicago club there in 1886 to "boil out."

He might be a lord surveying his realm, and if that's what **CHRISTY MATHEWSON**, *above*, is doing at the Polo Grounds in 1906, then he is absolutely correct. In his day Christy personified the image of New York baseball as Ruth and DiMaggio were to do for future generations. The New York ace also broke new ground for baseball at large, for his image included a cultured, well-spoken, quasi-aristocratic quality. There is indeed a sovereign expression in Mathewson's pose, in the strength with which he has anchored his legs, the dignity with which he holds his body, the authority with which he contemplates the borders of his realm.

But nothing that Mathewson did or said or represented would have been noted by history had he not possessed a potent arsenal of fastball, curve, and fadeaway (a screwball, in today's lexicon), each of which he delivered with masterly efficiency.

Facing Page: The young, strikingly handsome **CHRISTY MATHEWSON** is all business as he limbers up the right arm that carried him, John McGraw, and the New York Giants to fame and success during the first dozen years of the twentieth century. The relationship between McGraw and his ace is one of baseball's interesting stories. Not only did the sulphurous John J. get along professionally with his gentlemanly 30-game winner, but at one time they and their wives actually shared a New York City apartment. Considering the fact that some managers are uncomfortable at sharing even a dugout with certain of their players for a few hours, this arrangement suggests there might have been more to the profane and irritable McGraw, as well as to the aloof and self-possessed Mathewson, than mere anecdotes can tell.

If the pitching fraternity has a patriarchal figure it is **CY YOUNG**, in whose name each year's outstanding pitchers are honored with a coveted award. Cy's career ran from 1890 to 1911, spanning baseball's most decisive years of evolution. His real name was Denton True Young, the "Cy" deriving from someone's comparison of his fastball to a cyclone.

Cy's "unbreakable" records are 511 wins and 313 losses (when you pitch for 22 years you're going to lose a few). The reason he gave for finally retiring at the age of forty-four was not a lame arm but a big belly, the makings of which are becoming evident in this 1905 picture when Cy was with the Boston Pilgrims (later known as the Red Sox). "I had trouble fielding bunts, you see," he said. "The boys saw that and they just kept dropping 'em down on me. So I decided to quit. Was nothing wrong with my arm."

A man of longevity in every respect, Cy lived on until 1955, long enough to have seen all the golden arms: Walter Johnson, Lefty Grove, Bob Feller. "They were the fast ones," he said. "But I was right with them."

Well, an old man may tell some tales. But when a fellow wins 511 games, you listen.

JOHN ("STUFFY") McINNIS, *facing page,* and JACK BARRY, *above,* were, respectively, the first base and shortstop components on what probably is, after the Tinker-Evers-Chance combine, the most famous infield in baseball history. Where the Chicago Cubs trio gained their indelible celebrity through a piece of doggerel, the Philadelphia Athletics quartet won instant and lasting fame because of the dollar valuation their manager Connie Mack placed upon them: "The $100,000 infield." Connie wasn't talking about what he paid them (top stars like Wagner earned around $10,000 a year at the time), but in reaching for a sum that he knew would impress his contemporaries, said, "I wouldn't take $100,000 for them."

McInnis, Barry, second baseman Eddie Collins, and third baseman Frank ("Home Run") Baker played as a unit for just four years, 1911–1914, during which time the A's won the pennant three times. After the 1914 season, Mack, unwilling to meet the higher salaries demanded by his players, began breaking up the team. Collins was sold to the White Sox and Barry to the Red Sox, while Baker held out for the entire season. McInnis remained with the A's until 1917. For Collins, Mack received $50,000, at the time the largest cash transaction ever in baseball.

DANNY MURPHY, *above,* was one of Connie Mack's stalwarts on five Athletics pennant-winning teams between 1902 and 1913. A Philadelphia boy who grew up to play with the local club, Murphy hit the major leagues as a second baseman and played that position for the first eight years of his career, and by all accounts played it well. At that point the career of Danny Murphy becomes instructive: How does a second baseman become an outfielder overnight?

The answer is simple: If you're playing second base when Eddie Collins joins the team, you go elsewhere.

Those striped caps were distinctive to the Philadelphia Athletics, who wore them from 1909 to 1914; because they happened to coincide with so many winning seasons the caps remained associated with success in the minds of many old-time fans.

If he was as tough as he looked, then **CY MORGAN,** *opposite,* was not a man to trifle with—that face preaches a wordless sermon of no nonsense. Cy (his real name was Harry) was a right-handed spitballer who arrived in the major leagues with the St. Louis Browns in 1902 and later pitched for the Boston Red Sox. In 1909, a year before this picture was taken, he was traded to the Philadelphia Athletics and for three years enjoyed his most successful seasons, winning 16, 18, and 15 for the A's before a bad arm finished

him. On most pitching staffs Cy would have been a prominent fellow, but around him on that Athletics mound corps stood such exalted talents as Chief Bender, Eddie Plank, and Jack Coombs. In 1910, when he helped the A's to the pennant with 18 wins and a 1.55 ERA, Cy was not even rewarded with a start in the World Series, as Connie Mack allowed Coombs and Bender to pitch every inning of the A's' five-game victory over the Cubs. Perhaps this picture was taken just after Connie had apprised Cy of his plans.

Above: There are many traditions associated with the World Series, the handshake between opposing team leaders being one of them. Second basemen **EDDIE COLLINS** (*left*) of the Philadelphia Athletics and **JOHNNY EVERS** of the Boston Braves were certainly the cutting edges of their respective teams. They have come together at mid-diamond, caps in hand, to wish each other luck of sorts as the 1914 World Series prepares to open at Philadelphia's Shibe Park.

With those strikingly different uniforms, there was no difficulty in telling the teams apart. Evers' slightly wider smile is that of the winner-to-be, for his was the club known as "The Miracle Braves," who had made a run from last place in July to win the National League pennant and were about to pave the far superior Athletics under in four straight.

Facing Page: Bat on shoulder, Philadelphia Athletics outfielder **RUBE OLDRING** stands along the left-field foul line at New York's Hilltop Park one sunny afternoon in the summer of 1910. Behind him, the walls in left and left-center are adorned with advertisements, as the walls in many big league parks were. In later years some of these ads, like Brooklyn clothier Abe Stark's "Hit Sign, Win Suit" at the base of Ebbets Field's right field scoreboard, became famous for themselves.

Rube (who came by his nickname legitimately—he was not a backwoods bumpkin but a New York City boy named Reuben) was one of the solid men on Connie Mack's championship teams of the era. If Rube's uniform somewhat lacks the stylish look it can be attributed to the fact that as late as 1912 most players paid for their own uniforms; for around thirty dollars they got a suit of heavy flannels that shrank and otherwise did not take kindly to laundering, and thus were washed as infrequently as possible.

Page 42: Standing in front of the lathered-up Ever-Ready razor blade and Adams chewing gum ads is Philadelphia Athletics outfielder **AMOS STRUNK**, one of the more gifted defensive center fielders of his time. Amos played on all four of Connie Mack's pennant winners between 1910 and 1914. A part-timer in his early years, he got his chance at the end of the 1910 season when regular center fielder Rube Oldring broke a leg. Amos played in the Series that fall, did well, and was on his way to a solid seventeen-year career.

Suspending his common sense for a moment, one Philadelphia sportswriter said that the "luckiest" thing that happened to the Athletics was "Oldring breaking his leg, because it gave Strunk a chance to show what he could do." Oldring's opinion of this "lucky break" was not recorded. Strunk ultimately became the last living member of Connie Mack's great pre-World War I champions, dying in 1979 at the age of ninety.

Page 43: Connie Mack called his 5´5˝ outfielder **TOPSY HARTSEL** "my little towhead" for his white hair. His close-to-the-ground stature gave Topsy an advantage at home plate and Connie's leadoff man led the American League in bases on balls five times. Here he gives the photographer a bit of extra effort as he demonstrates the big league way of coming in on a fly ball. With the sun full in his face, Topsy (whose first name was Tully) looks as though he could have used a pair of sunglasses, but these were not then in use in the big leagues. The first man to use them reportedly was Boston Red Sox right fielder Harry Hooper, sometime during the World War I era.

Right: Wearing their bulky, casually buttoned sweaters, three members of Connie Mack's 1910 Philadelphia Athletics take a break in the sunlight. **HARRY DAVIS** (*left*), long-time first baseman and team leader, is nearing the end of a long career that has carried him across the threshold of the new century and through its first decade. Next to him is right-hander **JACK COOMBS**, known as "Colby Jack" for his attendance at that Maine institution, and soon to become even better known as a 30-game winner, aided and abetted by a glove that looks as if it was left in the oven too long. Then there is **EDDIE PLANK**, one of the most immaculately efficient left-handers ever. Like Coombs a college man, Eddie gained his higher education at the school in his native Gettysburg. Every year after the baseball season Plank returned to his hometown and worked as a tour guide on the famous battlefield, turning his thoughts from Ty Cobb and Walter Johnson to those of Robert E. Lee and Abraham Lincoln.

The white elephants on the sweaters are what a later age would call the team logo.

Page 46: If Honus Wagner was shortstop, then **TRIS SPEAKER** was center field. Until the advent of Joe DiMaggio and, later, Willie Mays, there was short discussion about who was in center on baseball's all-time all-star team: it was Speaker, flanked on either side by Ruth and Cobb. For years he was Ty's only legitimate rival as American League superstar, and indeed was the man whose .386 average in 1916 broke Cobb's skein of nine straight batting titles. It was one of the five plus-.380 averages in Speaker's career.

Shown here in 1912, Tris joined the Red Sox in 1907. In 1914, with the Federal League whispering money in his ear, he was able to squeeze a two-year $36,000 contract out of a grudging Boston management. When the Feds vaporized after two years, the Red Sox promptly trimmed Speaker's contract down to $9,000. When he refused to sign, he was sold to Cleveland, breaking the hearts of Boston fans, which put them in proper mode for the sale of Babe Ruth four years later.

An endorsement of Speaker the man came from teammate Smoky Joe Wood, Speaker's closest pal on the Red Sox: "The greatest thing that ever happened to me in baseball was having the friendship of Tris Speaker."

Page 47: When this picture was snapped in 1912, this slim, smiling young southpaw was at the very beginning of what was going to be one of the longest and most successful pitching careers in major league history. A Pennsylvania product, like so many of Connie Mack's players, **HERB PENNOCK** was destined to have his banner years not in Philadelphia but in Boston with the Red Sox and later, most glitteringly, in New York with the Ruth-Gehrig Yankees. Curiously loose-handed at times with his young talent, Mack let his twenty-one-year-old lefty go in 1915, the same year he let another future ace, Bob Shawkey, go to the Yankees.

Pennock, who pitched until 1934 and amassed 240 lifetime victories, was known as a clever "thinking man's pitcher." He was also extremely deliberate. When Yankee manager Joe McCarthy confronted him one day and said, "My wife says you're a 'noodle pitcher,'" Herb smiled at what he took as a compliment. "Yes," McCarthy went on, "she says she could cook a pot of noodles between your pitches."

Facing Page: It's September 6, 1912, at Boston's Fenway Park, then in its first year of operation. Red Sox fireballer **SMOKY JOE WOOD** is warming up before a crush of friendly onlookers. In those days ballparks were happy to sell more tickets than there were seats, herding the overflow behind outfield ropes or allowing them to hunker down on the grass in foul territory.

The reason for the large turnout at Fenway on this afternoon was an impending duel of titans. Earlier in the season Walter Johnson had set a record by winning 16 games in a row. On this afternoon Joe Wood is going for his 14th straight and will be opposed by Johnson himself. It was dramatic, historic, and more than sold out. Wood, 34–5 that year (Johnson was 32–12), aced out Walter by a score—fitting for the occasion—of 1–0. Wood then went on to notch two more wins, tying Johnson for the record, before losing.

It looks like in order to get into the ballpark in those days you needed a ticket and a hat, preferably a straw hat.

Above: Sitting in the visitors' dugout at Philadelphia's Shibe Park before the start of Game Two of the 1914 World Series are right-hander **BILL JAMES**, manager **GEORGE STALLINGS**, and right-hander **DICK RUDOLPH** of the Boston Braves, the "miracle team" that came from last place in July to win the pennant. The dugout, with its scratched, nailed-together plank walls and plain wooden benches, does not appear designed for comfort. The glove standing on its fingers next to Rudolph looks like a candidate for the ancient artifacts box, though you can be sure that it was regarded as an important piece of equipment by someone. Those are probably small blankets piled above it, which players used for warmth when the weather turned chilly.

Stallings was one of the few managers who chose not to suit up for a game (Connie Mack was another). Not long after having his picture taken, James got up from the bench and pitched a two-hit shutout.

Facing Page: This moment of suspended activity at Philadelphia's Shibe Park during the 1914 World Series is further evidence of baseball's truism that "nothing happens until the pitcher throws the ball." Boston Braves outfielder **HERBIE MORAN** and Athletics catcher **WALLY SCHANG** each stare patiently at the mound, where the pitcher is letting the baseball age a bit. Or perhaps, since Schang's mask is still on the ground, Connie Mack's "$100,000 infield" hasn't finished throwing their warmup ball around.

Moran joined the Braves from the Cincinnati Reds late in the season and helped the club make its memorable run to the pennant. Where Moran's career was relatively brief, Schang's was nineteen years long, and successful. Wally played on seven pennant winners with three different teams and was a world champion four times with the Athletics, Red Sox, and Yankees.

Here's a snappy double play combination that couldn't have been more unalike in their individual approaches to life. Boston Braves shortstop **RABBIT MARANVILLE**, who has just crossed the bag as he fired the ball to first base in a pregame workout, was as blithe a spirit as baseball has ever known. Diving fully clothed into a hotel fountain and rising from the water clenching a goldfish between his teeth was one of Rabbit's more storied stunts. His partner, **JOHNNY EVERS**, however, was known as an irascible snarler—his nickname, "The Crab," had nothing to do with a penchant for crustaceans but was rather a gloss on Johnny's sandpaper disposition. But what these men had in common was more important than what set them apart: Whether it was with grin or grimace, they could play a winning brand of big league ball, and never more so than in 1914, when they sparked the Boston Braves to their "miracle" pennant.

They are shown here in the midst of their miracle season, wearing their dark blue road uniforms on a visit to New York's Polo Grounds.

Above: Eighty years after he left the big leagues in 1913 after a brief, notably undistinguished career, and fifty years after his death in 1943, **CLIFF CURTIS'S** name began reappearing in the sports pages across the nation. It all went back to events that had taken place between June 13, 1910 and May 22, 1911, when the Boston Braves right-hander lost 23 consecutive decisions, setting the record for a pitcher having nothing to write home about. Cliff's mortification remained unsurpassed until Anthony Young of the New York Mets began his own long, unhappy climb toward that ragged mountaintop. Losing with metronomic regularity in 1992 and throughout much of the '93 season, Young's futility disinterred Curtis from history and carried him along as Young neared the record and then passed it with a few to spare (27 losses in a row), releasing Curtis from his long-maintained ignominy.

Here, however, Curtis confidently loosens up in the bright spring sunshine in 1910, unaware of what lay ahead, observed by a few uninterested Polo Grounds fans who didn't know they were watching a future celebrity.

Facing Page: **RUSS FORD** is doing what many pitchers claim they love most to do—swing the bat—even those who leave behind .209 lifetime averages. Though he did hit five triples for the Yankees in 1910, Ford was most noted for his pitching, particularly in his 1910 rookie season, when he was 26-6. Russ, whose big league career was brief—four full seasons before a jump to the Federal League in 1914—built his success on an illegal pitch, the emery ball. "Everybody thought it was a spitball," one contemporary said. (The spitter was then a legal delivery.) "But it was an emery ball. He had a hole in his glove and under it was a piece of emery paper. Then he wore a ring on his finger with a piece of emery paper wrapped around it. The ring was on a rubber band, and when he pulled it off, it went up his sleeve." Ford's doctored baseball had a tendency to sail and was hard to hit. Like most bats of the era, the one he's using here is barely tapered. Unfortunately for Russ, he never figured out how to bring in an emery bat.

Above: No, this is not an advertisement for White Rock table water or Bushmill's Irish whiskey; rather it is young Giants outfielder **TILLIE SHAFER** out alone in the Polo Grounds outfield in 1912 demonstrating a favorite photographers' pose of the time. Shafer was in the employ of John McGraw's Giants between 1909 and 1913, coming to New York when he was just twenty years old. He left baseball after the 1913 season and McGraw was no doubt sorry to see him go, for Tillie had just batted .287 and stolen 32 bases. Shafer's given name was Arthur Joseph, and how they made "Tillie" out of that has been lost to history.

Facing Page: Whether **JACK ROWAN** has actually just delivered a baseball or has gone through his motion to oblige the photographer, we don't know, but he has certainly given posterity a permanent look at his game face. The burly Cincinnati right-hander is standing with one foot inside the warmup circle at New York's Polo Grounds, by the looks of it having made an early appearance on the field. In those years and until well after World War II, starting pitchers warmed up in front of their respective dugouts, a practice more crowd-pleasing than today's way of doing it in the bullpens.

Rowan, who wears a dark blue uniform with bright red socks, pitched for the Reds from 1908 through 1910, when he won 14 games, his biggest year, and then was traded. He returned to the Reds in 1913 and retired a year later with a sore arm, just 28 years old.

Above: It's April 14, 1914, and the Philadelphia Athletics and New York Yankees are opening the season at the Polo Grounds, where the Yankees were in their second year of co-tenancy with the Giants. A's catcher **IRA THOMAS** (*left*) is doing the honors for his club (skipper Connie Mack, wearing street clothes, always remained in the dugout), while manager **FRANK CHANCE** is representing the home team. Chance, of Tinker-Evers-Chance fame, managed the Yankees in 1913 and 1914, each time to a seventh-place finish, which probably made him a bit nostalgic for his 1906 Cubs team, which won 116 games. The elevated trains beyond the ballpark afforded passengers brief glimpses of the proceedings.

If that opening date seems late by today's standards, it was normal for the time, with some seasons starting even later. Not only did they play eight fewer games, but years ago there were quite a few scheduled doubleheaders.

Facing Page: **BILL CARRIGAN'S** reputation for toughness was so widespread that one wonders if he really needed all of that gear to go behind home plate. Indeed, his nickname was "Rough." Bill played for the Red Sox from 1906 to 1916, the last four years as catcher-manager. As a manager he was quite successful, leading the club to two World Championships; after the second one, however, he retired to enter the banking business in Maine. After the sale of most of their star players in the early 1920s, the Red Sox fell on hard times, and in 1927 Bill was enticed back to his old job. But Carrigan was merely a good manager, not a miracle worker, and with the teams he had he finished exactly where any other skipper would—in last place.

Tough but fair, Carrigan was remembered by many of his players, including Babe Ruth, who broke in under Bill in 1914, as the finest man they ever played for.

Pages 60 & 61: He didn't hit with much power to begin with, and even if he smacked one right on the nose, that dead ball wasn't going to go very far anyway. So **MILLER HUGGINS** did what most batters did in those days: He choked up on the bat handle, far up, to the extent that he appears able to stroke the ball with either end of that stick. From the angle of Miller's skyward gaze, the ball he has just hit in this batting practice shot seems to be hovering somewhere over the infield, which is about as far as they go when you're only using half the bat.

Huggins, shown here as a St. Louis Cardinal second baseman in 1910, made his mark on baseball in the 1920s, when he managed the New York Yankees to six pennants.

Right: In this rare game-action picture, history's most successful hitter is about to bring his bat forward. **TY COBB** appears in perfect balance as he strides into the pitch. This photo, taken in 1912 at New York's Hilltop Park, finds the twenty-five-year-old Cobb at the very peak of his extraordinary twenty-four-year career—he had batted .420 the year before and would attain .410 this season. Note how far back catcher Ed Sweeney is for Tyrus, which, given Cobb's penchant for bunting his way on, was asking for trouble. Note also that Sweeney still disdains those newfangled shinguards, which may account for his respectful distance from the batter. Ed's nearly erect posture suggests there might be someone on base whom he suspects of larcenous intent.

No doubt many in that packed grandstand came that day to see exactly what they are watching now.

Pages 64 & 65: In gritty, slashing action, here is baseball's most lethal performer in what many believe is the game's most representational picture. **TY COBB** has been caught in one of his archetypical moments. He had been on second base, extending his lead by inches, his feral diamond instincts yearning toward third. Suddenly he broke. Yankees third baseman Jimmy Austin, playing in, as third basemen were wont to do in those bunt-happy years, moved back to cover the bag against baseball's most dynamic human cyclone. The canny Cobb headed for a corner of the bag, his spikes plowing up a sizzling spray of dirt, his clenched-teeth expression demonstrating the passionate energy with which he played this game. The base umpire—there were only two umpires in those days—rushes over to cover the play. Austin, meanwhile, makes sure his left leg is clear of those flashing spikes. According to photographer Charles Conlon, who snapped this memorable picture at New York's Hilltop Park in 1909, "The catcher's peg went right by Jimmy, as he was thrown on his face," meaning that Cobb upended the third baseman. For Conlon, this became the signature photograph of a brilliant forty-year career; for Cobb, it was just one of his 892 lifetime steals. But it tells us that Ty didn't just mark the record books—he made incisions.

Above: The man in the middle may have the look of a successful politician on election night, but actually he is **BARNEY OLDFIELD**, the well-known racing car driver. In 1910, Barney set the speed record when he drove his Benz at nearly 132 miles per hour (the record stood for 13 months). Here he has slowed down long enough to relax in a Chicago restaurant with a couple of local heroes, **JOHNNY EVERS** (*left*) and **FRANK CHANCE**. Where the ballplayers seem interested in the baseball, Barney is making sure the camera is getting his full attention.

These are the saddest of possible words—
   "Tinker to Evers to Chance"
Trio of Bear Cubs and fleeter than birds—
   "Tinker to Evers to Chance"
Ruthlessly pricking our gonfalon bubble,
Making a Giant hit into a double,
Words that are weighty with nothing but trouble—
   "Tinker to Evers to Chance."

Facing Page: **JOE TINKER** was the front man on history's most famous double play combination, thanks to Franklin P. Adams's hastily turned out bit of poetry. Joe had a long, solid career as a major league shortstop, most of it spent with the Chicago Cubs. The Tinker-Evers-Chance unit enjoyed an unusually long tenure in the Cubs infield—1902–1911. Although Tinker and Evers synchronized smoothly around second base, they never talked about it. After a 1905 fistfight, they did not speak to one another off the field for more than three decades.

Pages 68 & 69: Addie Joss, one of the great pitchers of the era, died suddenly at the age of 31 of tubercular meningitis on April 14, 1911. The Cleveland Indians right-hander was held in such esteem by everyone that later in the season an **AMERICAN LEAGUE ALL-STAR TEAM** was put together to play the Indians in a benefit game for Addie's widow. And quite a team it was, featuring seven future Hall of Famers.

The All-Stars, *front row from left to right*: Second baseman Germany Schaefer, outfielder Tris Speaker, outfielder Sam Craw-ford, manager Jimmy McAleer (of the Washington Senators), outfielder Ty Cobb (in a borrowed uniform), and catchers Gabby Street and Paddy Livingston. *Back row, left to right*: Shortstop Bobby Wallace, third baseman Frank "Home Run" Baker, pitchers Smoky Joe Wood and Walter Johnson, first baseman Hal Chase, outfielder Clyde Milan, pitcher Russ Ford, and second baseman Eddie Collins.

The All-Stars won the game, 7-2.

Of **HONUS WAGNER**, one writer said, "He is to shortstops what Shakespeare is to Elizabethan playwrights." A far reach, no doubt, but you get the idea. There are those who took it even further: They called him the greatest ballplayer who ever lived.

Wagner came to the big leagues in 1897 as an outfielder, then over the next few years played first base, third base, second base, and all outfield positions. It wasn't a case of finding a suitable spot for him, it was simply that he was so proficient wherever they put him that a manager was tempted to play him everywhere. The greatest shortstop of all time—the designation is one of baseball's few undisputed dicta—didn't become a regular at the position until 1903.

Here is Honus, bundled up on a chilly day in 1914, selecting his bat from an array that appear remarkably alike. The fact was that in those days the circumference of a bat hardly varied from top to bottom. Honus swung them all with great purpose, winning eight batting titles and at one time or another leading the National League in almost every category.

In creating athletic icons, posterity is grudgingly selective, demanding more than just statistics. Well, Wagner had that extra. He was a folksy, lovable character; modest, whimsical, a spinner of tall tales. An American original.

Above: A pitcher's arm, baseball men will tell you, should be trim and limber, without undue bicep development, enabling it to wheel and snap like a whip. The right arm of **JACK COOMBS** certainly appears to fit this preference as he sits for a photograph that was assuredly not his idea.

Jack seems to be regarding his pay wing with a certain dubious detachment, as if wondering why, after treating him to 60 victories in 1910 and 1911, it suddenly lost its magic and forced his descent to the ranks of ordinary baseball mortals. But for all of that, it remains decidedly a pitcher's arm, with a baseball at the end of it.

Facing Page: Looking hauntingly alone as he prepares for a game in the Brooklyn Dodgers clubhouse at Ebbets Field, **JACK COOMBS** is a man in thoughtful contemplation. He's almost ready, needing only to lace up his spikes and put on his blouse and cap. Does the absence of other players indicate that Jack is early, or are his teammates already out on the field?

This picture was taken in 1916, when Coombs, then 33 years old, was drifting further and further from his few years of stellar glory with the Philadelphia Athletics. Jack had won 31 games for

Connie Mack in 1910 and 29 the next year. Soon after, illness and injury reduced him from spectacular to average pitcher and he moved on to Brooklyn, where he toiled with modest distinction for four years.

Compared to today's large, carpeted, splendidly lighted and appointed clubhouses, those in Coombs's day were spartan and strictly functional. Players were hardly pampered by their employers back then.

Above: Baseball's most prestigious nickname belonged to **JOHN FRANKLIN ("HOME RUN") BAKER**. Although he led the American League in home runs four times during the dead-ball era (his high was 12), Baker gained his nickname for a pair of crucial four-baggers he hit against the Giants in the 1911 World Series. Frank was the third baseman on Connie Mack's munificently named "$100,000 infield." Connie later sold him to the Yankees.

Facing Page: Baseball is a serious game, especially when you are re-viewing the ground rules before the opening of a World Series. The Series in question is the 1915 edition, between the Philadelphia Phillies, managed by **PAT MORAN** (*left*), and the Boston Red Sox, managed by **BILL CARRIGAN**, whose expression seems designed to illustrate his nickname of "Rough." Moran, at whose Shibe Park the game was to be played, no doubt knew the strictures by heart and appears less interested than Carrigan.

Here is Baker the proud and loving father as he poses with his daughters Ottlie (*left*) and Janice at the Polo Grounds in 1921, a year before his retirement from the big leagues. Frank had missed the entire 1920 season to be with his girls after the death of his wife.

One of the strongest players of his time, Baker is said to have swung a 52-ounce bat, which is about 20 ounces heavier than the average bat used today.

The Phillies won the opener behind Grover Cleveland Alexander, then were swept in the next four, destined not to win another World Series game for sixty-five years. In 1950 they went down in four straight to the Yankees, but finally in 1980 they beat the Kansas City Royals in six games, giving the franchise what is thus far its only world title.

Left: Umpire **BILL KLEM** (*left*) watches as Giants manager **JOHN McGRAW** (*center*) and White Sox skipper **CLARENCE ("PANTS") ROWLAND** give each other a less than enthusiastic handshake before Game Three of the 1917 World Series at the Polo Grounds. Klem, behind the plate that day, appears a bit swollen up by his inside chest protector. Behind them, a man with a megaphone announces the lineups, which is the way it was done in the days before PA systems.

McGraw, whose teams won ten pennants, never had much luck in World Series play, winning only three times; the White Sox won this one in six games. Rowland was fired after the 1918 season, which wasn't the worst thing that could have happened to him: The White Sox club that won the pennant in 1919 decided not to try to win the World Series.

Pages 78 & 79: Meet the outfield of the pennant-winning 1916 Brooklyn Dodgers, posing at Ebbets Field in the tic-tac-toe uniforms the team wore that year. From left to right, they are **CASEY STENGEL, JIMMY JOHNSTON, HY MYERS,** and **ZACK WHEAT.** Players were not expected to take the field in spanking-clean uniforms in those days, with Myers taking the practice to perhaps extreme lengths.

"Casey always had something to say, even in those days," recalled Boston Red Sox right-hander Ernie Shore, who pitched against the Dodgers in the 1916 World Series. Before the opener, Stengel passed Shore and a few other Boston players in the outfield during batting practice and said to them, "Hello, boys. What do you think your losing share is going to come to?" The Sox players laughed at him. They knew they had the better team and proved it, dispatching Casey and his mates in five games.

Above: Looking like an apparition that just glided down from the silent screen, Mrs. **SHERROD SMITH** poses with her husband, whose occupation then was left-handed pitcher for the Brooklyn Dodgers. Despite the spectral elegance of her finery, Mrs. Smith does not seem particularly overdressed, if we take note of the other well-groomed fans who have turned out early this afternoon at Brooklyn's Ebbets Field.

Smith, a solid journeyman pitcher for the Dodgers and later the Cleveland Indians, pitched some splendid games in World Series competition, losing to Babe Ruth and the Red Sox 2–1 in 14 innings in the 1916 Series, and, in the 1920 Series, beating Cleveland 2–1 on a three-hitter and then later losing 1–0 to them.

Facing Page: Yes, he used that thing in a game and yes, it was legal. It's **HEINIE GROH'S** famous "bottle bat," designed by him, unique to him. The barrel was large and untapered, the handle thin. It probably made bunting, a tactic at which Heinie was quite adept, easier. He used his singular bat to compile a lifetime batting average of .292 for 16 years of big league toil between 1912 and 1927, a career he divided between the Reds and the Giants. Groh's finest moment came in the 1922 World Series, when his .474 batting average helped the Giants beat the Yankees. After that, the proud Groh drove around in a car with a "474" license plate.

Back in those less genteel days Indians were known as "Chief," Southerners as "Reb," and if you were of German extraction, well . . .

"Who are you calling 'Shoeless'?"

JOE JACKSON might be thinking that as we direct our attention to his rather elegant-looking, ankle-high, shiny leather footwear, *left*.

Joe, a member of the Cleveland Indians (for whom he toiled from 1910 to 1915), is doing here what he did best—easing back on his left foot and cocking that black bat, which, it was said, he swung with more innate poetry than any man of his time. The facts are on Joe's side: He batted .408 in his rookie season; then, hit by the sophomore jinx, slid to .395 the next year.

He has been drawn as the game's Noble Savage. Baseball's "most natural hitter" ever could neither read nor write. Joe's response to his ragtag intellectual image was: "I ain't afraid to tell the world that it don't take school stuff to help a fella play ball."

Ironically, it is the soiled image of the compromised man from the 1919 World Series that accompanies the legend of the game's purest swing. Joe and his fellow conspirators were drummed out of baseball in 1921 and consigned to a twilight beyond its universe.

Above: Here are two baseball veterans who might be reflecting on the game's caprices. **WILLIAM ("KID") GLEASON** (*left*), after a long playing career, had the joy, in his first season as a big league manager, to lead his Chicago White Sox to the league championship, only to watch a group of his players collude to throw the World Series. At right is the team's one-time super pitcher **ED WALSH**, who pitched with such lionhearted devotion that he burned himself out by the age of thirty-one. After some drifting about here and there, including a brief stint as an American League umpire, Ed returned to the White Sox as a coach, when this picture was taken.

Facing Page: It seems like a lazy summer's day as **LENA BLACK-BURNE** (*left*) and **CHICK GANDIL** get ready for that afternoon's game against the Yankees at Hilltop Park. The year was 1910, nine years before the moody Gandil, a first baseman, sank into infamy as one of the alleged ringleaders of the 1919 Black Sox. Blackburne, a utility infielder who played at the big league fringes for a few teams, was destined to make an unusual contribution to his favorite game. It was on his farm near the Delaware River that he discovered and later marketed the special mud that is used by umpires to rub the gloss off of new baseballs before a game. Gandil also had some mud for the game, his being of the figurative kind.

Right: The great **ED WALSH** appears warmly avuncular as he embraces fellow Chicago White Sox pitchers **JIM SCOTT** (*left*) and **EDDIE CICOTTE**. After six years of averaging 375 innings per season, Big Ed's arm finally gave out in 1913. Scott, who threw a spitter and a screwball, was twice a 20-game winner for the Sox. He served in France in 1918 and did not return to the big leagues after the war. Cicotte won 29 games for the White Sox in 1919 but is remembered today for being one of the villains of that year's World Series scandal, for which he was booted out of baseball.

The White Sox wore those black uniforms for road games from 1902–1916. Ironically, it was the 1919 team that became known as "The Black Sox."

Pages 88 & 89: Here is a man who opted to live by his own code of honor and paid dearly for it. He is **GEORGE ("BUCK") WEAVER**, the lone "innocent" member of the eight White Sox players pitched out into the cold because of the 1919 World Series scandal. Weaver's sin was knowing about the plot and not reporting it, which was sin enough when the offense was brought before Judge Landis, who had a one-way-street view of purgatory. Despite his pleas for reinstatement, Buck never made it back.

Weaver was considered one of the finest third basemen of his time and was just thirty years old when he was drummed out of the corps, leaving on the high note of a .333 batting average, his best season. Buck's tragedy is a cautionary tale: Be careful with whom you associate, be careful about what you hear, and be careful about what you don't tell.

Sitting on the bars behind the batting cage during the pre-game workout, Chicago White Sox pitchers **EWELL ("REB") RUSSELL** (*left*) and **EDDIE CICOTTE** await their turns to enter the cage and have their rips. Russell, a left-hander, had several effective years for the White Sox before a dead arm finished him in 1919, the year that Cicotte and a half-dozen of his mates dumped the World Series. Russell made an unusual comeback in 1922 as an outfielder with the Pittsburgh Pirates. He batted .368 and in 60 games drove in 75 runs. He hit well the next year, then retired for keeps.

Russell hailed from Jackson, Mississippi, and with the Civil War then still part of living memory, he, like many Southern players, found himself tagged with the nickname "Reb."

1920-1939

Pictures of **BABE RUTH** in solitary contemplation are rare. For one thing, history's greatest slugger was not given to internal consultation but was rather an intuitive, raucously spontaneous character; and for another, this fellow seldom had the chance to be alone, for on the field or off, Babe Ruth was the most magnetic American of his time. He exuded an aura that was both welcoming and endearingly ingenuous.

It didn't take Ruth long to be impelled from the periphery into the very heart of baseball, a game that he single-handedly elevated to new levels of popularity. His arrival in New York in 1920 marked the beginning of the Yankee dynasty, which he continued to help perpetuate and prosper even after his retirement. For years and years talented youngsters would turn down offers from other teams and sign with the Yankees because, as one of them, Tommy Henrich, said, "I wanted to play where Babe Ruth played."

If Babe Ruth had not lived, it would have been impossible to invent him. In 1917 the one-time incorrigible bad boy of the streets of Baltimore was a twenty-four-game winner for the Boston Red Sox and the best left-hander in the game. By 1919 he was an outfielder, setting a new single-season home run record, which he broke in 1920 and again in 1921 with a sky-high total of fifty-nine. In image and achievement he was gargantuan. Not in the farthest extremities of imagination would any Hollywood scriptwriter have dared conceive him. In everything—slugging, eating, drinking, womanizing—he was prodigious. He was loud, coarse, uninhibited, ingenuous, and beloved beyond any

athlete in history. Wes Ferrell, ace pitcher of the 1930s, summed it up succinctly and definitively: "Babe Ruth was baseball."

Ruth's arrival on the scene was a triumph of timing. Shaken by the scandals of the 1919 World Series, the game needed a positive shock to its system, and along came Ruth to excite and mesmerize with adrenaline-racing feats of long-distance power shots, abetted by a livelier ball that made it a hitter's game.

Thanks primarily to Ruth and the excitement he generated, by 1921 most American League teams had set new attendance records. The age of Cobb, of bunt and slash for runs, was over. Abetting the hitters in the home run and line drive mayhem they were committing on the baseball diamonds were an array of new rules. The spitball and other freak deliveries were outlawed (with dispensation allowed for a handful of veteran pitchers who relied heavily on the spitter). A ball that became even lightly scuffed was thrown out of the game, forcing pitchers to work with tight, shiny new balls that were more difficult to grip.

While the baseball establishment never admitted that anything had been done to liven the ball, the fact was that after the war a better brand of yarn from Australia had become available, and this yarn was wound tighter by improved machines. It all helped account for the stratospheric batting averages that glitter through the 1920s, for not

Left: Not to worry, that's pitcher **RAY CALDWELL'S** non-pitching hand the Yankee trainer is tending to. Caldwell, who featured the spitball, pitched for the Yankees from 1910 through 1918.

The Yankees adapted their famous pinstripes as home uniforms on a permanent basis in 1915, and although the fabric has long been identified with the club, they weren't the first to wear it; pinstripes were worn in the National League as early as 1907.

Above: This isn't just a crowd of celebrity seekers surrounding the Babe, but more a congregation of idolizers and worshipers, brightly thrilled and excited at being within the radiance of their hero. For these cloth-capped youngsters it was a dream-fulfilling and unforgettable moment. And the man at the core of it all, dapper in his bow tie and straw hat, appears no less delighted than the least of them, pleased at the joy he is able to circulate.

every hitter was taking Ruthian rips at home plate; the truth was, most were not. The players of the 1920s had all learned their game in the dead-ball era, when, because there was no point in taking haymaker swings, you choked up on the bat and poked at the ball—contact, not distance, was your intent. Employing this style of hitting against the lively ball produced hailstorms of base hits and created a "Golden Age of Hitters." Things got so lusty that in 1922 Cobb batted .401 but still finished a distant second to George Sisler's .420. Between 1920 and 1929, eleven men batted .380 or better, yet didn't lead the league.

If Ruth was the supreme monarch of the home run, then the top machine gunner of base hits was the St. Louis Cardinals' Rogers Hornsby, whose batting averages from 1921 to 1925 read like the reveries of an aspiring sandlotter: .397, .401, .384, .424, .403. Along with Ruth and Hornsby, the decade produced names that are like the paving stones of a baseball Valhalla: Sisler, Harry Heilmann, Al Simmons, Paul Waner, Jimmie Foxx, Lou Gehrig. The decade also turned out the team whose very mention still resonates with all-time greatness: the 1927 Yankees, with an assassin's lineup that featured Ruth at his sixty–home run summit, hitting back-to-back with his crown prince, Gehrig.

This was as close as black youngsters could get to organized baseball in the 1920s. NORMAN ("KID") ELBERFELD, manager of the Southern League's Little Rock club, chats with a couple of baseball-happy kids who are taking obvious delight in being where they are. The young man on the left is Archie, the other is Red, and Elberfeld used them to help warm up pitchers—indeed, that's a catcher's mitt Red is wearing on his left hand as he holds up a well-traveled baseball in the other. Elberfeld's pair of irregulars were good enough for the skipper to take on road trips with the club.

All of the hitting finally culminated in one shattering detonation in 1930, when the National League compiled a .303 batting average and the American League .288. Offensive records were established that have never been broken. Pitchers became an endangered species. It was like a fireworks celebration of, and farewell to, the pinwheeling, big-spending decade of Prohibition, speakeasies, hyperventilating stock markets, and postwar surges of buoyant optimism and self-indulgent cynicism. It was a national binge, as if we knew that it was to be the century's last unthreatened decade, before economic depression, world war, and a nuclear age that would abide no miscalculations.

Abashed by the ludicrous run totals of 1930, the game drained a bit of the bounce from the ball in 1931, restoring most of the game's checks and balances. "It was amazing how the pitching improved in one year," said right-hander Burleigh Grimes with dry sarcasm.

As the national economy began to fall apart, as banks failed and industries collapsed, baseball, with a kind of stubborn ingenuousness, persevered, remaining a pillar of stability amid the surrounding concussions. Not a franchise collapsed, not a game was missed. Babe Ruth, Jimmie Foxx, and Hank Greenberg blasted soaring home runs in mammoth totals, while Lou Gehrig, as if performing some act of faith and continuity from one era to the next, put together his remarkable record of 2,130 consecutive games played.

Above, left: Relaxing in the Brooklyn Dodgers clubhouse is ace right-hander **VAN LINGLE MUNGO**, one big, strong, hardthrowing pitcher, whose misfortune it was to spend most of his years working for losing teams. In his mid-1930s prime they said that no one in the National League, not even Dizzy Dean, delivered the ball faster than Mungo.

Above, right: "I joined the Cardinals in 1923," third baseman Les Bell recalled in later years. "Naturally, I was scared and nervous. **JIM BOTTOMLEY** came over to me and put his arm around me and said, 'Just take it easy, kid, and you'll be fine. And if you make any low throws across to first base, don't worry, kid, old Jim will scoop them right up for you.'

"Well, that helped me," Bell said. "But when I look back on it now, I've got to laugh. I was twenty-one years old at the time, and 'Old Jim' was all of twenty-three."

Facing Page: When this picture was taken in 1934, **DAZZY VANCE**'s decade with Brooklyn is behind him and he is on the payroll of the Cincinnati Reds.

Page 100: Top row, left to right: **MULE HAAS,** .300-hitting outfielder. Sharp-hitting out-fielder **EARL AVERILL,** was one of the most popular players in Cleveland history. **TED LYONS,** White Sox ace with 260 wins. *Center row, left to right:* **VAN LINGLE MUNGO,** who seems up to a bit of mischief here. **AL LOPEZ,** superb National League catcher; later a winning manager in the American League. **"WILD BILL" HALLAHAN,** hard-throwing Cardinal left-hander. *Bottom row, left to right:* **BUDDY MYER,** Washington's .300-hitting second baseman. **RED ROLFE,** the line-driving Yankee third baseman. **SPUD CHANDLER,** who compiled a .717 winning percentage for the Yankees. *Page 101: Top row, left to right:* The Giants' **BILL TERRY,** the National League's last .400 hitter. **HARRY DANNING,** New York Giants catcher in the 1930s. **CY WILLIAMS,** home run hitting Phillies outfielder of the 1920s. *Center row, left to right:* **RUDY YORK,** Detroit's power-hitting first baseman. **MICKEY COCHRANE.** Everyone agreed: He was "fiery." **LEFTY GROVE,** perhaps the greatest of all left-handers. *Bottom row, left to right:* **JOE McCARTHY,** one of the most successful of all managers. Yankee rookie **DIXIE WALKER,** later a Brooklyn favorite. **TONY LAZZERI.** A tough hitter, but remembered mostly for one strikeout.

Baseball continued doing what was most important to its perpetuation—turning out those lodestone stars around whom the game gathers. There was Dizzy Dean, fastballing right-hander of the St. Louis Cardinals, whose cornpone charm and engaging braggadocio seemed to sustain the verities that were threatening to sink into the national morass. In 1936 the Yankees introduced Joe DiMaggio, the sleekest and best-armed ship of state ever to cross the high seas of major league baseball; that same year the Cleveland Indians sent to the mound an electrifying seventeen-year-old right-hander named Bobby Feller, whose fastball traveled through the fast lanes hitherto reserved for Walter Johnson and Lefty Grove. And at the decade's end, the Red Sox unveiled the snapping, poetically pure left-handed swing of Ted Williams, an intensely focused youngster whose ambition was to be nothing less than the greatest hitter of all time—an ambition that in the opinion of many he fulfilled.

On May 24, 1935, the Cincinnati Reds, overcoming the skepticism of the other clubs, introduced night ball to the big leagues. General Manager Larry MacPhail's innovative move, derided as an "experiment" and a "fad" by most of the game's entrenched doyens, soon caught on and by the end of the decade other teams began installing light towers on their own grandstand roofs. The most memorable introduction of night ball came at Ebbets Field on June 15, 1938, when Cincinnati's Johnny Vander Meer turned in one of sport's most sublime individual achievements by pitching a second consecutive no-hitter.

On August 26, 1939, another momentous occasion slipped quietly into the chronicles. On that afternoon, which again saw the Reds and Dodgers meeting in Brooklyn, television cameras were present for the first time in a big league park. "Before two prying electrical eyes," the *New York Times* reported the next day, major league baseball had "made its television debut." Television set owners, the story went on, "as far away as fifty miles viewed the action and heard the roar of the crowd."

With dynamic new stars and technological advances, the future of America's game never seemed brighter. Unfortunately, it was the world around it that was turning darker.

  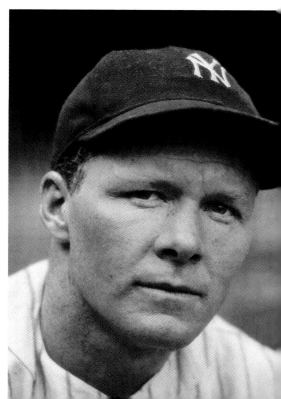

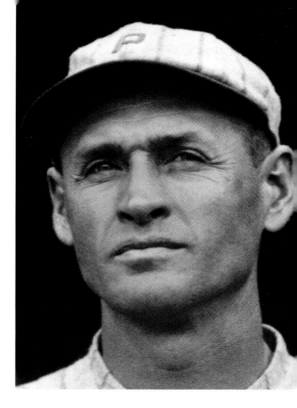

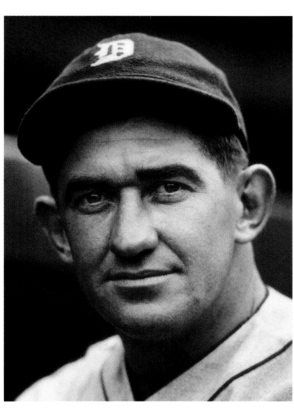
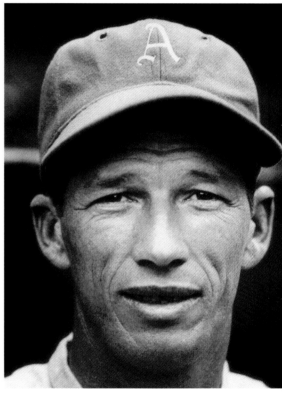

Two of the men who helped build baseball into a national institution during the century's first two decades take a quiet moment together at New York's Polo Grounds. Giants manager **JOHN McGRAW** (*left*) is in conversation with the man he considered the greatest of all players, Pittsburgh's **HONUS WAGNER**, then at the end of his long playing career. Honus seems to be having a deep and wistful look into the past, his large hands holding that bat with tender affection.

Once upon a time the game's titans almost automatically became managers, either during or late in their careers, among them Ty Cobb, Tris Speaker, Eddie Collins, Walter Johnson, Rogers Hornsby, and Nap Lajoie. In 1917, his last year as an active player, Wagner was handed the job of managing the Pirates, but after six games he decided the job was not for him. Perhaps McGraw is asking him why.

Above: New York Giants manager **JOHN McGRAW** (*right*) welcomes his one-time ace and personal favorite, **CHRISTY MATHEWSON**, back to the Polo Grounds. The year is 1919 and Christy is recently back from military service. An American hero to the tips of his fingers, Christy had, at the age of thirty-eight, joined the army's newly organized Chemical Warfare Service. He inhaled some mustard gas during a training session in France that damaged his lungs, and may have weakened them to the point where he became vulnerable to the tuberculosis that took his life in 1925.

When he returned from France, Mathewson was out of a job and McGraw quickly hired him as a coach. But Matty's once robust physique was deteriorating and he remained with the Giants just one year. Soon after, Mathewson moved to Saranac Lake, New York, a small Adirondack Mountain village where Dr. Edward Livingston had established a sanatorium for TB sufferers. There, among the dark green forests and shining lakes, baseball's "gentleman hero" awaited the end.

Facing Page: It is one of baseball's most charming stories. In 1925, when sixteen-year-old **MELVIN THOMAS OTT** came up from Louisiana to be inspected at the Polo Grounds by John McGraw, his delivery label was marked "catcher." McGraw asked the youngster if he had ever played the outfield.

"When I was a kid," the shy, polite Ott said.

McGraw remained poker-faced. He liked this boy. And he liked him even more when "Master Melvin" entered the batting cage and began whipping a bat with as natural a swing as John J. had ever seen. Ott hit everything, despite a most unorthodox batting style—the left-handed-hitting youngster would lift his right

foot high off the ground as the pitcher delivered, hold it aloft for a moment, then plant it as he swung, with never any disruption of his timing.

Ott remained with the Giants for twenty-two years, one of the most popular players in New York baseball history. He managed the team from 1942–1948, without much success. His reserved, evenhanded approach to the job evoked Leo Durocher's famous dictum: "Nice guys finish last."

Here is Ott in 1929, still just twenty years old, the year in which he hit 42 home runs, posing in front of a slightly cracked Polo Grounds dugout wall.

Above: There were two truly outstanding brother combinations in the big leagues in the 1920s, Pittsburgh's Waner boys and New York's **MEUSEL** brothers. In the case of the latter, however, the brothers toiled on different teams, **EMIL** (*left*) for the New York Giants and **BOB** for the New York Yankees. Emil, known as "Irish," was the older by three years. Here he visits Bob at the Polo Grounds, the home field their respective teams shared until 1922.

Bob Meusel was known for an extraordinarily powerful throwing arm and an extremely reticent disposition which made him unpopular with sportswriters. Irish had a reputation for being devastating in the clutch. When asked how his old teammate was able so frequently to respond to pressure, Freddie Lindstrom said, "Irish was a good low-ball hitter and often in those situations, with the winning run parked out there, the pitcher will throw breaking balls and try to keep them down. And that was right in Irish's alley."

The brothers, each of whom was a lifetime .300 hitter, faced each other three times in World Series competition, from 1921–23, with Irish's Giants winning the first two.

Facing Page: When Dixie Walker was in his heyday as a smooth-swinging .300-hitting outfielder with the Dodgers in the 1940s, he was known at Ebbets Field as the "People's Cherce," which was Brooklynese for affectionate popularity. A generation before, the people of Brooklyn had had another "Cherce," an outfielder named **ZACK WHEAT**, who gave the fans eighteen years of faithful, highly efficient service in left field.

Zack was a shy, mild-mannered Missourian who joined the Dodgers in 1909 when he was twenty-one years old and immediately began hitting line drives to all corners of the yard.

"Zack was one of those ballplayers," an old-time sportswriter said, "who you only had to look at standing out there on the field to know he was an exceptionally decent fellow. The fans sensed it right away and they developed an affection for him that never waned."

Here is Zack in batting practice, showing some of that precision of form that Dodger fans cherished for nearly two decades.

Above: "I knew him when he was hitting grand slam home runs," said Bill Dickey, Gehrig's closest friend on the Yankees, "and I knew him when he was dying. He was always the same. He never blew his own horn and he was never sorry for himself."

LOU GEHRIG was in the Yankees lineup on June 1, 1925, and many a branch would stir in the night before he was out of it again; not, in fact, until May 1, 1939. In this photograph of Gehrig, sitting in the dugout later in the 1939 season, it's all history, and what lay ahead was two years of slow, muscle-atrophying death from amyotrophic lateral sclerosis, known informally today as "Lou Gehrig's Disease."

Here Gehrig, alone as a man can be, stares wistfully out at the field he once so splendidly performed in. For all athletes the twilight must come; for Gehrig it was more than that.

Facing Page: LOU GEHRIG did it all—home runs, triples, doubles, runs batted in, batting average—and he did it without interruption for 14 years, across 2,130 consecutive games. He was without ego or temperament, was in fact so mysteriously internal in his mechanical efficiency that he seemed almost without personality. Yankee pitcher Spud Chandler said of his great teammate, "I was on the team for two years before he spoke to me. Was he unfriendly? No, I wouldn't say that. He was Gehrig, that's all. It's the way he was."

Among left-handed power hitters, only Ruth and Williams are in Gehrig's class. But as a sports icon he remains singularly unique, a paragon of modesty, dependability, consistency, and, finally, tragedy.

Pages 110 & 111: Speaking in later years, pitcher Waite Hoyt said of his old teammate BABE RUTH, "Believe whatever you hear about him. I don't care what the story is, how unlikely or incredible, you can believe it. That's the way he was."

Here is Ruth in the act of contributing to that incredible and unlikely legend. It is Game Four of the 1926 World Series at St. Louis's Sportsman's Park, and Ruth has just unloaded in the first inning. The Babe is looking deep; he knows it's gone, as do catcher Bob O'Farrell and umpire Bill Klem. Ruth homered twice more in this game, becoming the first man ever to take the trot three times in a single Series game.

The master showman was always primed for baseball's biggest show, hitting 15 home runs in the 36 World Series games he started as an outfielder.

In the 1928 Series, Ruth again hit three home runs in a single game against the Cardinals in St. Louis. After the third one, the enthralled Cardinal fans began throwing their hats out onto the field in tribute.

Pages 112 & 113: You can never be quite sure if they're really fans or not, but it certainly never hurts the presidential image to turn out for a World Series game. (Woodrow Wilson, in 1915, was the first sitting president to attend one of these pageants.)

Backed up by a swarm of politicos, **CALVIN COOLIDGE** adds some presidential mystique to the proceedings as he prepares to throw out the first ball of Game Three of the 1925 World Series, played on October 10 at Washington. Enjoying the occasion are (*far left*) Mrs. Coolidge and Pittsburgh Pirates manager Bill McKechnie, while Washington Senators manager-second baseman Bucky Harris stands at the other side of right-hander Coolidge, with Judge Landis peering over Harris's shoulder.

The black armband on McKechnie's left sleeve is in memory of Christy Mathewson, who had died three days before.

Facing Page: **WILBERT ROBINSON** managed the Brooklyn Dodgers for so long (1914–1931) that the team became known as "The Robins" during his tenure, and long after his retirement some newspapermen still referred to the team as "The Flock."

"Uncle Robbie" was easygoing and good-natured, a portly, sometimes absentminded skipper who was the perfect foil for the collection of blithe spirits he handled in the 1920s, whose antics and exploits earned the club still another nickname: "The Daffy Dodgers."

When catcher Val Picinich joined the team in 1929 he felt he wasn't getting enough playing time and broached the matter with the skipper. Uncle Robbie gave him the facts.

"I don't know how to spell your name," the skipper said.

"Why don't you let somebody else make out the lineup card?" Picinich said.

"That's a good idea," Uncle Robbie said appreciatively.

Page 116: **MIKE GONZALEZ**, a rookie up for a cup of coffee with the 1912 Boston Braves, models the latest in catching gear. If the mask seems barely able to defend Mike's profile against a whistling foul tip, then the chest protector seems designed to let you know just exactly how hard the ball is hitting you. It makes one wonder whether catching in those years was a position or a penance.

Nevertheless, catchers survived, including Mike, who was still at it as late as 1932, which suggests that that equipment was sturdier than it appears.

When his playing career came to an end, the Havana-born Gonzalez became a scout for the St. Louis Cardinals. It was in this capacity that Mike, who always had a chancy relationship with the English language, coined one of baseball's most succinct scouting reports. Sent out to evaluate the talents of a player who turned out to be snappy of glove but light of stick, Mike filed the following appraisal: "Good field, no hit."

Page 117: There is not, as it seems perhaps there ought to be, a specially landscaped sylvan glade for 40-game winners to go to upon retirement. There have been only two of these magnificent beasts of burden in the twentieth century: Jack Chesbro (41–13 with the 1904 Yankees) and **ED WALSH** (40–15 with the 1908 White Sox). Looking slightly ill at ease, as though he might have been dragooned into this costume, is Walsh, shown here as an American League umpire in 1922. That Big Ed stayed in the job for just a single season before returning to uniform as a White Sox coach tells us he was not entirely comfortable in it.

Wanting to remain in the game, former players did occasionally make the transition that at one time would have seemed inconceivable and became umpires. When his career ended in the 1930s, former Yankees pitcher George Pipgras became a Man in Blue. When he was asked what he had learned about umpiring that he had never suspected as a player, George said, "I learned that umpires never make mistakes."

Above: After a fine career as a winning pitcher, sidearming right-hander **HOWARD EHMKE** was pulled unexpectedly from the shadows by Connie Mack for one last sunburst of glory. It occurred in the opening game of the 1929 World Series. Bypassing his aces Lefty Grove and George Earnshaw, Mack selected Ehmke to start against the powerful-hitting Chicago Cubs, the idea being that Howard's assortment of soft curves would baffle the predominantly right-handed-hitting Cubs lineup. Ehmke had won only seven games that year and his selection perturbed his Philadelphia Athletics teammates.

But Ehmke proved that Mack had learned something during his 43 years in baseball. Keeping the Chicago sluggers off stride all afternoon, the veteran right-hander set a Series record (since broken) by fanning 13 and pitching the A's to a 3–1 victory, sending his club off to what was an eventual World Championship.

The following season Ehmke got into just three games and then was gone—but not before Connie had gotten all that was left.

Facing Page: It was not because of any abating of his blazingly competitive drive that finally forced **TY COBB** to retire. "My legs wouldn't carry me anymore," Tyrus said ruefully. Fly balls that once upon a time he would have inhaled with ease were dropping untouched in his sector, and the one-time blue streak of the base paths no longer went from first to third in the blink of an eye.

When he was released by the Detroit Tigers in 1926 after twenty-two years, the last six as player-manager, Cobb signed on with the Philadelphia Athletics. He batted .357 and .323—

admirable for a man in his forties—but it was becoming harder and more frustrating for the older man to play the younger man's game.

After retiring as an active player, Cobb never returned to baseball. He didn't have to; through a series of shrewd investments during his career, including a large block of Coca-Cola stock, he had become independently wealthy. Ty, shown here in 1928, demonstrates the hands-apart grip he used at home plate for much of his career. He claimed it helped him place the ball where he wanted it to go. With a .367 lifetime average, nobody argued.

Above: When they were in the field, Philadelphia Athletics players always kept glancing toward their dugout, just in case their skipper might be instructing them to take some tactical step back, forward, or to the side. When skipper **CONNIE MACK** delivered his bit of semaphore he generally did it with little flicks of his scorecard, as he is demonstrating here.

Very early in his managerial career Connie decided to forgo wearing a uniform, thereby creating his own distinctive aura at the ballpark. He was not allowed to leave the dugout during the game and if there was some dispute on the field the umpires often came over to the dugout to explain to "Mr. Mack" the basis for a decision.

In time, Mack's gentle, seemingly eternal presence earned him the status of some sort of secular saint. Most of his players admired and respected him and counted themselves lucky to have played for Mr. Mack. Connie may have led the ideal American life. He reached the major leagues as a catcher in 1886 and didn't leave until 1950, when he retired as manager of the Philadelphia Athletics at the age of eighty-eight, having spent every summer's afternoon for sixty-four years watching a baseball game.

Facing Page: For a generation of baseball fans, who knew him as a tall, distinguished beanpole of a gentleman who evoked respect from everyone from batboys to Presidents of the United States, it might come as a shock to realize that **CONNIE MACK** didn't always have white hair, didn't always look like the village patriarch, that in fact he once was young. Here is the proof—Connie soon after the turn of the century, in the early years of his fifty-year tenure as manager of the Philadelphia Athletics, the team he later became majority owner of.

Connie, who earned the eternal thanks of linotype operators when he pared his name down from Cornelius McGillicuddy, left behind the kind of record inevitable for someone who stays around for just short of forever. He had magnificent teams—some of the greatest ever—and won nine pennants, but he also fielded some of the least persuasive, at one time finishing in last place for seven consecutive years. But he never lost his zest for the sport, and he was always a sympathetic employer: Owner Mack could never find it in his heart to fire Manager Mack.

Above: St. Louis Cardinals manager **BILL McKECHNIE** (*left*) sits in the dugout behind a battery of baseball cannons. His companion in this study of mutual solitude is **GROVER CLEVELAND ALEXANDER**. The year is 1928 and Alex is now 41 years old, with magic enough left to win 16 that year, his last productive season. It's just about all in the books now for Alexander, including his grandest, culminating moment, the now-mythic strikeout of the Yankees' Tony Lazzeri with the bases loaded in the seventh inning of the seventh game of the 1926 World Series, the turning point in the Cardinals' championship victory. This classic generational conflict between the rookie Lazzeri and the veteran Alexander caught baseball's collective imagination and has long assumed the dimensions of bas-relief sculpture.

After enduring brutal artillery bombardments in World War I, Alexander returned home a soul-shattered man, an alcoholic and given to epileptic seizures. A haunted loner, Alex's face shows all the harsh inroads. The following season McKechnie, a kindly and understanding man, had to let him go because of unreliability.

Facing Page: There is nothing in the rule book about having to be spotlessly upholstered before you can play in a World Series, and here is pictorial evidence. These three St. Louis Cardinals outfielders are in Yankee Stadium getting ready to play in the 1926 World Series against the New York Yankees. They are (*left to right*) **BILLY SOUTHWORTH, TAYLOR DOUTHIT,** and **CHICK HAFEY**. Having helped the Cardinals to their first pennant, the three are exuding pride and confidence as they get set to step foot on baseball's biggest stage. The confidence was not misplaced, as they defeated Babe Ruth's Yankees in seven games.

Those two redbirds poised on either end of a sloping bat, one of baseball's most famous team symbols, first appeared on Cardinal uniforms in 1922.

Above: Next to Babe Ruth, **DIZZY DEAN** was probably the best-known baseball player of his time. There was something engaging about his exploitation of personality opposites: loveable braggart, shrewd country bumpkin. Dizzy, whose first name was Jay (sometimes he said it was Jerome), is shown here (*right*) with his younger brother **PAUL**, a quiet, reserved young man who was forced to labor under the nickname "Daffy." The brothers were fastballing right-handers with the St. Louis Cardinals in the 1930s, most notably the 1934 World Champion "Gas House Gang" club, for whom Dizzy won 30 games and Paul 19.

The glory of the Deans was brief, each succumbing to arm injuries, Dizzy in 1937, when he was 26 years old, and Paul in 1936, when he was 23.

Facing Page: Neatly dressed for their day at the ballpark, one of them with the beanie cap which some youngsters affected at the time, a group of boys has suddenly struck gold—the great **DIZZY DEAN** has agreed to come over and autograph their scorecards and scraps of paper, thereby turning those items into priceless mementos. The smallest boy has climbed to the top of the railing in order to witness the actual scrawl of the pen. Dizzy seems patient and unhurried, indifferent to the fact that for each of these boys this would forever be an ageless moment, stolen from time and crafted into sweet memory.

Left: If you doubt that baseball is indeed a serious game, just have a look at these three members of the St. Louis Cardinals, convening in their dugout for some studious appraisal of the pregame limbering up. They are (*left to right*) outfielder **PEPPER MARTIN**, catcher **MICKEY OWEN**, and pitcher **LON WARNEKE**. The picture was taken in 1939, the year that all major league teams wore those centennial patches on their left sleeves. Baseball, which was rather self-conscious about the murkiness of its origins, had declared 1839 as the year of its "invention," hence the patches.

Two of these men are remembered in World Series history: Martin, whose hitting and base-stealing led the Cardinals to victory over the Philadelphia Athletics in 1931, and Owen, whose muff of a last-out third strike in the fourth game of the 1941 Series led to a Brooklyn Dodger loss to the New York Yankees.

Pages 128 & 129: Chicago Cubs manager **JOE McCARTHY** (*right*) welcomes some quite distinguished visitors to his dugout. Along with coach **JIMMY BURKE** (*left*) is writer **RING LARDNER** (*hat in hand*) and Broadway ace **GEORGE M. COHAN**. The year is 1929.

The dour-faced Lardner was a longtime sportswriter, novelist, short story writer, and playwright, known for his caustic humor and on-the-money satire. His short novel, *You Know Me, Al,* is one of the few classics of baseball literature. Cohan, who wrote and performed such standards as "Over There" and "Give My Regards to Broadway," was vividly portrayed by James Cagney in one of Hollywood's most popular efforts, *Yankee Doodle Dandy.*

Burke, just about lost to history now, had a lyrical nickname that no doubt appealed to the creative gentlemen at his left: "Sunset Jimmy."

Above: Baseball is a young man's game, but it also has its patriarchal figures who lend it dignity and stability. Here are two of them: **JUDGE KENESAW MOUNTAIN LANDIS** *(left)*, who, as its first commissioner, is credited with restoring the game's integrity after the Black Sox Scandal. With him on this chilly day at the ballpark is **CONNIE MACK,** who was present on the big league scene as player and manager from 1886 to 1950. Connie holds one of those scorecards with which he waved his players into position during a game.

Facing Page: He was baseball's avenging angel, the man who was enthroned as its first commissioner by the game's magnates in 1920 to restabilize their industry after the foundation-shaking revelations of the Black Sox and other scandals. **JUDGE LANDIS** was granted absolute power and he wielded it with great flourish. He became so indelibly identified with baseball's integrity that the club owners, who eventually tired of his dictatorial ways, were still unwilling to unseat him, and Landis remained at his post until his death in 1944.

Landis enjoyed going out to the ballpark and watching the game from a front-row box, often in the pose seen here. His full name was a walloping Kenesaw Mountain Landis, after a Civil War battlefield in Georgia where his surgeon father was wounded. It is a most unusual name, but perhaps the judge was fortunate that his father was not wounded at Spotsylvania Court House.

Facing Page: One of the strongest men ever to play big league ball, **LEWIS ("HACK") WILSON** stood 5´6″ and weighed a muscle-packed 190 pounds, meaning he was quite a compact energy mass. For a few years he made the most of it. Playing for the Chicago Cubs, he led the National League in home runs four times, most thunderously in 1930, when he set the league record with 56 and, more impressively, the major league standard with 190 runs batted in, a figure that no one comes even close to anymore.

But Hack's residence on those Olympian heights was a strictly short-term lease. The small, powerful man (his nickname derived from George Hackenschmidt, a professional wrestler noted for his physical strength) had a weakness for booze and operated almost totally without self-discipline. His decline was sudden and precipitous, from 56 home runs to 13, from 190 RBIs to 60. The Cubs got rid of him after the 1931 season and Hack spent his last few years toiling for the Brooklyn Dodgers.

Page 134: When that leg came down there appeared from behind it a baseball that was traveling as fast as any human being has ever thrown it. **BOB FELLER'S** speed was described as "terrifying," and his curve as so lethal it should have been outlawed. He was to the fastball what Ted Williams was to hitting—the definitive symbol.

Here, in 1937, he is still just eighteen years old, a year after he electrified America's favorite sport by breaking into the big leagues with strikeout records. He remains the only genuine prodigy in baseball history. In later years he was asked if he had ever been nervous on the mound. Feller, who in fact had been a composed and unusually mature youngster from the very beginning, answered, "No. I was never nervous standing on a pitching mound. Why should I have been?"

Indeed. When you can throw a baseball in excess of 100 miles per hour, one supposes that any twitching of nerve ends is occuring sixty feet away.

Page 135: **LEFTY GOMEZ** pitched for the New York Yankees from 1930 to 1942, during which time the club won seven pennants and six World Championships. It was also the era when the Yankees fixed in place their image of corporate efficiency, personified by manager Joe McCarthy's all-business approach, Joe DiMaggio's poker face, and Lou Gehrig's stolid dignity. Among this sober fraternity the whimsical, witty Vernon Gomez was fresh air itself. A consistent winner on the mound, away from it he was breezy and irreverent, not above tweaking even the great DiMaggio, who admired Lefty and envied his poking wit.

Lefty's most memorable lines came from the twilight of his career. When asked if he was throwing as hard as ever, he said yes, he was, "but the ball isn't going as fast." When asked about his prescription for success, he said, "Clean living and Joe DiMaggio in center field."

Pages 136 & 137: The 1932 Chicago Cubs infield, (*left to right*) third baseman **WOODY ENGLISH**, shortstop **BILLY JURGES**, second baseman **BILLY HERMAN**, and first baseman **CHARLIE GRIMM**, shows us how they stopped batted balls from getting through, and they did it well enough that year to help bring a pennant to Wrigley Field. Grimm took over as manager from Rogers Hornsby in August that season and guided the club home to the pennant. Always a favorite in Chicago, Grimm had three different tenures as Cubs skipper.

Notice that the Wrigley Field outfield wall is not yet decorated with its now-famous ivy covering, which was planted soon after the 1932 season. The idea was to beautify the park and return to baseball something of the pastoral look associated with its origins. The ivy is popular with everyone except those outfielders who have to dig through the vines to extricate a batted ball.

Barnstorming baseball teams were a familiar sight on the green diamonds of America before the days of television. Big league players often organized postseason all-star teams and toured the country. In addition, there were numerous semipro teams riding the buses, following the highways and the back roads to take on the locals in Sunday doubleheaders. Among the most famous of these travelers were **THE HOUSE OF DAVID**, a club whose gimmick was bearded players (facial hair was then banned in professional baseball).

The heyday of the House of David was in the 1930s, and briefly among their number at the time was Grover Cleveland Alexander (appearing in a false beard), who attracted a few fans as he tossed his soft curves over the plate and then reboarded the bus for another journey to nowhere.

On the facing page we see two members of the club watching their bearded colleagues in pregame workout, in a setting that is definitely not big league.

1940–1947

".406" and "56" have come together for a moment in the dugout, tools of the trade in hand. We don't know what the conversation is about, but, given his chief line of interest, Ted might have been talking about hitting, and Joe might have been thinking, "I know all about that."

In their time they were Mr. and Mr. Baseball, subjects of many a passionate discussion predicated upon that timeless baseball poser: Who would you rather have? Either answer would be 100% correct.

An intrepid writer once put the question to the man who had managed each in their primes.

"When I managed the Yankees," Joe McCarthy said, "I was crazy about DiMaggio. When I managed the Red Sox, I was crazy about Williams." Then he sighed and said, "How the hell are you going to answer a question like that?"

World War II left behind, among many other things, permanent blank spaces in the records of Ted Williams, Bob Feller, Joe DiMaggio, Hank Greenberg, and hundreds of other players. These statistical deprivations will forever tantalize those for whom the record books have scriptural allure.

But before they left, after the 1942 season, two of those players turned in performances that have become benchmark feats in professional sports. Joe DiMaggio would of course be indelibly engraved in the game's annals even without his fifty-six-game hitting streak in 1941, but it was that gripping and exciting flight through one-third of the season that has assured his halo of stardust.

Also in 1941, Ted Williams, making a mighty leap toward fulfilling his grandiose ambition of becoming the greatest of all hitters, completed his third big league season with a batting average of .406, seeing it through with a bravura flourish on the season's last day. Going into a doubleheader, Williams was batting .3995—rounded off, an even .400. Disdaining the opportunity to sit it out and take his precious crown safely home with him, Williams played in both games of the doubleheader, hit safely in six of his eight at bats, and raised his average to .406, a figure that has since stood in clear and isolated splendor alongside DiMaggio's "56" (leaving baseball fans the eternal debate as to which was the more stellar accomplishment). It earned for Williams the accolade that has continued to ring impressively through the rest of the century: the last man to hit .400.

Unlike 1917–18, this time the major league rosters felt the heat of world war. With the nation reeling from the shock of the Pearl Harbor attack and its entry into what promised to be a long, perilous fight for survival, there was some talk of baseball closing down for the duration. The notion was patriotically motivated, but even at times of direst crisis it was possible to be excessively patriotic, as no less a baseball fan than President Franklin D. Roosevelt was to point out. In a January 15, 1942, letter to Commissioner Landis, the president wrote:

> I honestly feel that it would be best for the country to keep baseball going. There will be fewer people unemployed and everybody will work longer hours and harder than ever before. And that means that they ought to have a chance for recreation and for taking their minds off their work even more than before.

If ever a sport had its national significance defined, this presidential affirmation on behalf of baseball was it. Roosevelt's letter was front-page news across the country. And so the game, along with the rest of wartime America, geared up to face come what may as best it could.

After the 1942 season the big league rosters began to undergo severe depletion as more and more players left for military service. Like the

The rain is no deterrant to the fans who lined up outside Yankee Stadium for their World Series tickets in the early 1950s. The Yankee juggernaut had by this time turned this into an annual event, and would continue to do so. The tradition of October baseball for the club had been started by Mr. Ruth and his colleagues back in 1921. When Yankee talent finally began to lose steam, more than a generation had passed. Out of a possible forty-four American League pennants between 1921 and 1964, Yankee teams won twenty-nine. So, protecting themselves from the rain with newspapers, umbrellas, and raised topcoats, these fans are determined not to miss out on the autumn ritual.

automobiles of those rubber-shortage years, teams rolled forward with retreads and desperate patch jobs. Stocked with military rejects, veterans extending their careers, players hauled out of retirement, and various suspects and pretenders, the game went ahead.

The lasting symbols of wartime ball are left-hander Joe Nuxhall, hired by the Cincinnati Reds a few weeks before his sixteenth birthday, and the one-armed outfielder Pete Gray, pressed into service by the St. Louis Browns. In 1944, the Browns, who had never in their history won a pennant and who had long been synonymous with baseball futility, underlined the game's ragged wartime experience by winning the American League pennant. For any bemused baseball purist who asked incredulously, "The *Browns*?" the answer was that familiar dark year's phrase: "Don't you know there's a war on?"

But the war would not last forever, and one man in baseball knew that better than anyone else. Branch Rickey, newly hired president and general manager of the Brooklyn Dodgers, was looking ahead. It was the innovative Rickey who, while running the St. Louis Cardinals in the 1920s and 1930s, had devised the farm system, doing it so well that the players he steadily developed were to bring nine pennants to St. Louis between 1926 and 1946. Now Rickey had another plan, one so controversial and revolutionary that he dared confide it to no one outside his immediate family.

Rickey had long been troubled by organized baseball's color barrier, an injustice he felt would no longer be tolerated in the postwar world. Under the guise of putting together a team that would represent Brooklyn in the then-operating Negro League, Rickey had his scouts begin scouring the country for black talent. The man Rickey had in mind, however, had to have dimensions beyond just being able to run, hit, and throw. He was looking for a man of intelligence, vision, and unbreakable resolve. The man he found in the late summer of 1945 was then playing shortstop for the Kansas City Monarchs.

In October 1945, the Montreal Royals, an International League club that was then Brooklyn's top farm club, announced the signing of Jack Roosevelt Robinson, a superb twenty-six-year-old all-around athlete from California.

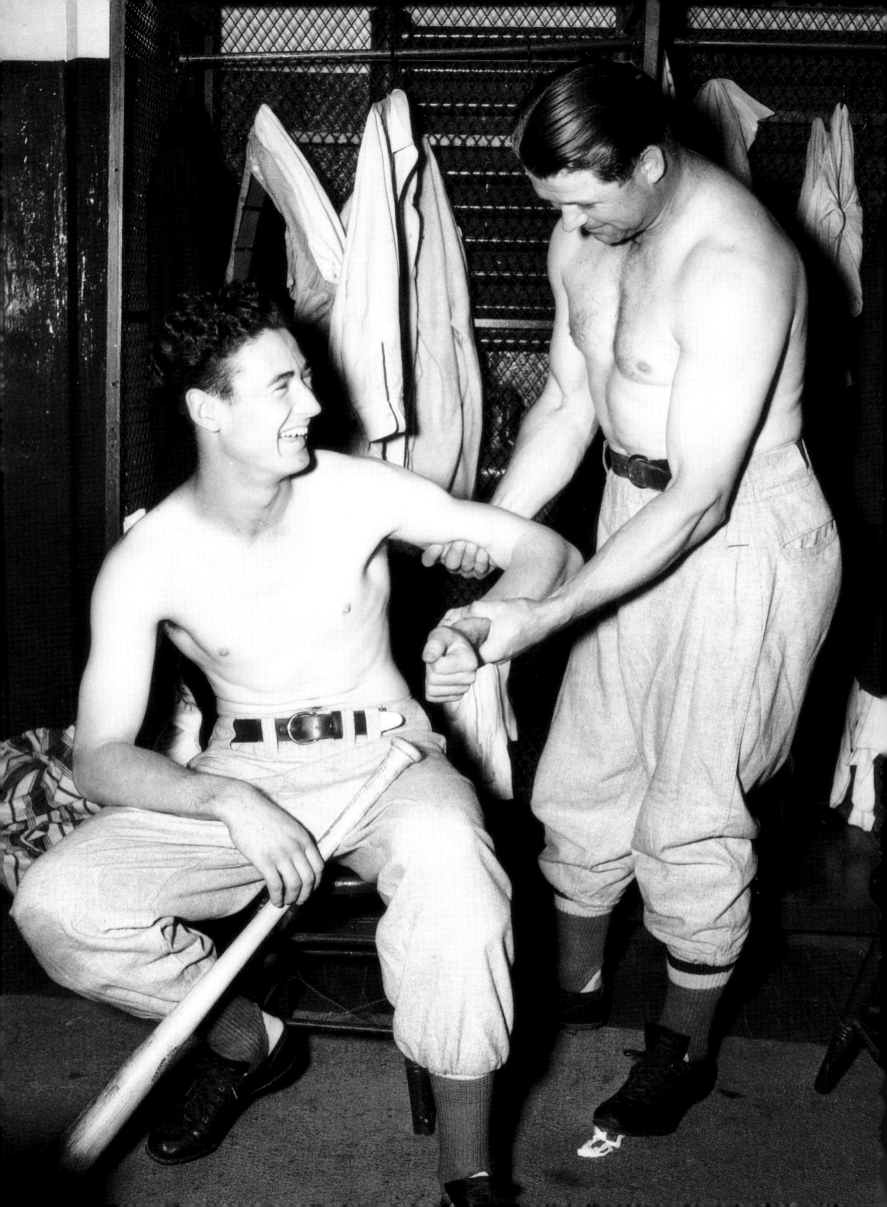

Facing Page: **TED WILLIAMS'S** passionate interest in hitting wasn't confined to his own efforts; he was intrigued by anyone who swung the bat well, as is indicated here by the intense interest he takes in a teammate's practice rips.

Williams studied pitchers with the same intensity he did hitters. It was a science to him, this game, this almost primal instinct of striking a ball with a stick, and as in any discipline, the man with the most cogent knowledge had the advantage.

Early in his career, Williams was talking to Ted Lyons, the fine pitcher who had entered the American League in 1923. Suddenly the young slugger asked the magic question: "Do you think I'm as good a hitter as Babe Ruth?"

Lyons said, "Well, wait till you get dry behind the ears. You've only been in the league a few years." But when Lyons realized how serious Williams was about this, he gave a truthful answer: "Of course you're as good a hitter as he was."

That Rickey had shown the foresight and courage to take this step went largely unappreciated by his fellow baseball executives. Rickey later said that a secret report passed among the fifteen other major league owners unanimously condemned his plan to integrate America's game. But it didn't matter. Nothing mattered, because it had begun, and after that it was Robinson's gritty resolve, blazing talent, and steely self-discipline that carried it forward.

Robinson was not just a gifted baseball player, but spectacularly so. He batted .349 for Montreal in 1946 and the following spring was promoted to the Dodgers, whom he galvanized to the 1947 National League championship.

No other player had ever come to the big leagues under such pressure and with such large demands placed upon him. Forbidden by Rickey to respond to beanballs, spikings, and the mindless racial invective hurled at him, the naturally militant, combative Robinson kept his temper in check, all in the name of "the cause," as Rickey had preached it to him.

Rickey had chosen his man well. It is hard to imagine another athlete with the talent, personal magnetism, and vision of the future that Robinson possessed as he used the base paths of the big league diamonds to relentlessly chart the way to a more equitable baseball America.

Page 148: Top row, left to right: **JOE GARAGIOLA,** St. Louis Cardinals catcher, and a good one. **HARRY BRECHEEN,** crafty Cardinals southpaw known as "The Cat." **FRENCHY BORDAGARAY,** outfielder and free spirit. *Center row, left to right:* **FRANK CRESPI.** The Cardinals second baseman was nicknamed "Creepy." **PHIL CAVARETTA.** A Chicago Cubs favorite for two decades. **EDDIE WAITKUS,** the first baseman who is remembered for having been shot by a deranged female fan. *Bottom row, left to right:*

BILL NICHOLSON, Cubs slugger and two-time National League home run and RBI leader. **LUKE APPLING** of the White Sox. No shortstop has ever batted higher than his .388 in 1936. **PAUL DERRINGER.** One of the top pitchers of the 1930s and early 40s. *Page 149: Top row, left to right:* **TOMMY HENRICH,** the popular Yankees outfielder known as "Old Reliable." **BUD METHENY,** who was part of the Yankees' wartime outfield. **DUTCH LEONARD,** ace knuckleballer of the Washington Senators.

Center row, left to right: **NICK STRINCEVICH,** an ace on Pittsburgh's wartime staff. **RIP SEWELL,** the man who invented the high-arcing "eephus" ball. **VITO TAMULIS,** left-hander for the Yankees in the 1930s. *Bottom row, left to right:* **GEORGE METKOVICH,** journeyman outfielder for six different teams. **KEN KELTNER,** the Cleveland third baseman remembered for the fine plays that helped end DiMaggio's 56-game hitting streak. **PAUL WANER.** The Pirate star won three batting titles.

Standing behind the batting cage at Yankee Stadium, **TED WILLIAMS** can't help taking a practice rip. He did it everywhere: on the field, in clubhouses, even in hotel rooms, where he watched himself in the mirror, because as important as it was to hit home runs, it was just as important to look good doing it.

Williams's obsession with hitting was, in the opinion of Red Sox manager Joe Cronin, detrimental to his fielding, in which the young slugger showed little interest. Watching Williams in the batting cage one day, Cronin expressed his lament to general manager Eddie Collins (who had scouted and signed Williams for the club).

"All he wants to do is get up to the plate," Cronin said.

"Well, Joe," Collins said, "wouldn't you—if you could hit like that?"

Facing Page: **CHARLIE KELLER** loosens up as he awaits his turn at bat during an exhibition game at the Yankees' St. Petersburg, Florida, spring training site. When he first joined the Yankees in 1939, the New Yorkers had swept to a fourth straight pennant, and the cry throughout baseball was, "Break up the Yankees." The team then swept the Cincinnati Reds in a four-game World Series, with Keller leading the way with three home runs and a .438 batting average. "Never mind the Yankees," Cincinnati fans said ruefully. "Just break up Keller."

Above: Standing in front of his locker at the Yankees' St. Petersburg spring training camp in 1941, outfielder **CHARLIE KELLER** is stripping off after a workout in the tropical sunshine.

Pages 154 & 155: **JOE DiMAGGIO** completes one of the mightiest swings in baseball. "Elegance" and "grace" and "style" inevitably attend word portraits of the Yankee center fielder, and to convey the fullness and the execution of his talent there are no better choices, be he at the plate, in the field, or on the bases. At home plate he was a precisely controlled dynamo of fury: bat cocked high, feet planted wide, perfectly still until the final moment, when he advanced his left foot a mere inch or two and turned loose one of baseball's thunderbolt swings. His eye was uncanny. This picture was taken in 1941, the year of his 56-game hitting streak; the hard-swinging DiMaggio struck out just 13 times in 541 official at bats.

Note that at the time this photograph was taken, photographers were still permitted on the field, and rather close up, too.

Page 156: It couldn't have been easy being Joe's younger brother, but **DOMINIC DiMAGGIO** never let it bother him as he put in a fine eleven-year career in center field for the Boston Red Sox, where, it is said, he could even out-Joe with his glove. Dominic was three years younger than the family titan, five inches shorter, and twenty-five pounds lighter. "The Little Professor" (so called because he wore glasses and was a serious young man) did labor under some misguided comparisons early in his career. When he was playing in the Pacific Coast League, some scouts passed on him, saying he "only hits singles," as though, like minnows, singles are thrown back. But when you're batting in front of Ted Williams, as Dominic was throughout his career, they are precious, and Joe's brother hit enough of them to compile a .298 lifetime batting average.

Page 157: **JOE DiMAGGIO,** shown here in 1937, during the second year of the career that would elevate him to the status of American legend. He is one of the few ballplayers—fellow Yankees Ruth and Gehrig are others—whose names have transcended the game and established themselves in the national culture. Spiced by his brief postcareer marriage to Marilyn Monroe, DiMaggio's mystique remains, six decades after his debut upon the green pastures of Yankee Stadium, uniquely enduring.

Above: It is a bright, sunshine-drenched July 4, 1939, at New York's Yankee Stadium; but the day is a poignant one. **LOU GEHRIG,** shown here with **BABE RUTH,** is making his farewell appearance on the field where he created his mighty legend. One of the most mod-est and reserved of all the game's heroes, Gehrig, who at this point had less than two years to live, said that while he might have been given "a bad break," he nevertheless considered himself "the lucki-est man on the face of the earth."

Facing Page: **BABE RUTH** the player was long retired by the time this mid-1940s photograph was taken, but Babe Ruth the legend went on and on, always ready to greet his fans and his old friend the camera. Here he is paying a royal call at Yankee Stadium—"The House That Ruth Built"—in his camel-hair cap and coat, cigar in hand, police protection needed to keep his devoted fans at bay.

Outside of a brief stint as a coach and batting-practice attrac-tion for the Brooklyn Dodgers in 1938, baseball never had a post-retirement job for its greatest name and most compelling symbol. Ruth died of cancer in 1948, just fifty-three years old. But as one of his old teammates said, "There were at least a dozen full lifetimes packed into those fifty-three years."

Facing Page & Above: Probably the most famous of all Negro League players was the tall, slender, fastballing right-hander **LEROY ("SATCHEL") PAIGE.** An engaging, whimsically philosophical character ("Age is a question of mind over matter. If you don't mind, it doesn't matter") Satchel pitched all over the map of Negro baseball for twenty years. Major league players who faced him in postseason barnstorming games said he was the equal of any pitcher in the big leagues.

In 1948, when he was 42 years old, Satchel received a dollop of belated justice when he was signed by the Cleveland Indians. The veteran player showed a flash of what-might-have-been by posting a 6–1 record and helping the Indians to the American League pennant. He remained on the big league scene until 1953.

Pages 162 & 163: **THE HOMESTEAD GRAYS,** shown here in the early 1940s, were one of Negro baseball's strongest and most successful teams. Negro League schedules were drawn up to allow the clubs to engage in games with white semipro teams, the best known of which were the Bushwicks of New York City. Carrying with them the magic of Josh Gibson and first baseman Buck Leonard, the Grays were the biggest drawing card on the circuit. Their Sunday doubleheaders at the Bushwicks' Dexter Park often drew well in excess of 15,000 fans.

"We draw big league crowds," Gibson once noted, leaving the rest unsaid.

Above: That's heavyweight champion **JOE LOUIS** holding the child. The year is 1937, and Joe is spending some time with his Brown Bomber softball team. In 1935, Louis organized and provided all of the funding for the team, which consisted mainly of boyhood friends. He paid for the uniforms and for the bus they toured in, and, when he was able to spare the time, traveled with them to help the gate: Joe was a draw at the ballpark as well as in the ring.

Facing Page: What Satchel Paige was to Negro League pitchers, **JOSH GIBSON** was to hitters—the powerful catcher of the Homestead Grays was known as "the black Babe Ruth." Though the records are skimpy and ill-kept (when they were kept at all), they show Gibson leading the league in home runs ten times between 1931 and 1946.

When Jackie Robinson finally broke the color line in organized ball in 1947, Gibson was both elated and bitter—pleased that the odious barrier had at last been dissolved, but pained that he, at the age of thirty-five, had fallen just short of benefiting from the great breakthrough.

PETE GRAY, shown here with his parents in 1945, remains the most evocative memory of baseball and World War II. When just a boy, Pete reached through the spokes of a farmer's truck just as the truck was put in motion. The mangling the youngster's arm received was so severe it had to be amputated at the shoulder. Pete's love for baseball, however, remained as fervent as ever. He soon developed a remarkable dexterity for catching the ball with his gloved left hand, pressing the ball against his chest, ridding himself of the glove, and seizing and throwing the ball before it fell. At the plate he had a strong, one-armed swing.

As baseball's wartime talent began to thin out, Pete made it into the pro ranks. Playing for Memphis in the Southern Association in 1944, he batted .333, stole 68 bases, and was voted the league's MVP. Even in watered-down competition this is good work; for a one-armed man, it was astonishing.

Gray reached the majors with the St. Louis Browns in 1945. Getting into 77 games, he slapped the ball around for a .218 batting average; perhaps unimpressive, but surely an inspirational triumph of will.

Facing Page: "**PETE REISER** just might have been the best baseball player I ever saw." The author of those words was Leo Durocher, who saw them all from the late 1920's on (and who also managed Willie Mays). There was nothing that "Pistol Pete" couldn't do on a ball field, and do to excess. He could play infield and outfield, he could switch-hit (though he batted almost exclusively left-handed most of the time), he had a strong throwing arm, could hit with power and for average, and he was never outrun by anybody. He was a batting champion at the age of twenty-two in 1941, his first full season in the major leagues. What he lacked on a ball field was luck. He was damned and doomed by the injury demon, from beanings at home plate to broken bones, and, most seriously, head injuries from running into outfield walls (which were solid concrete in those days). The injuries impaired and then finally wrecked what should have been one of the game's most glittering careers ever.

Pages 170 & 171: No one, on the field or off, has ever made richer, more lasting contributions to the game (and business) of baseball than **BRANCH RICKEY**. As a turn-of-the-century American League catcher, Branch was a washout, as he also was later as a manager. But once he got rid of his uniform and got behind a desk—here in the Brooklyn Dodger executive suite—Rickey got down to some serious work.

He is credited with introducing the concept of the farm system, which he began as general manager with the St. Louis Cardinals in the 1920s. And of course he is most remembered as the man who finally had the courage to take the giant step in 1945 of breaking baseball's long-institutionalized color barrier. He also contributed such tidbits as mandatory helmet-wearing for batters, which has not only prevented many a headache but saved many a career and possibly a few lives.

He was a trained lawyer, a classical scholar, a Biblicist, a visionary, and a man who could spot a good arm a mile away.

GIL HODGES left behind many persons for New York baseball fans to conjure. He was the smooth-fielding, home run–hitting first baseman on the incomparable Brooklyn Dodger pennant-winning teams of the 1950s; he was baseball's "strongest man"; and finally, he was the skipper who in 1969 led the New York Mets to the most improbable pennant and World Championship in baseball history. But Hodges was also a superb all-around athlete, a player of versatile, highly refined skills. He first came to the major leagues as a third baseman, then switched to catcher and was prepared to settle in there and begin his career, but along came Roy Campanella and Gil was moved once more, this time to what became his permanent location at first base, where he excelled with glove and bat for more than a decade.

Facing Page: If Tinker, Evers, and Chance had their poem, then **WARREN SPAHN** (*left*) and **JOHNNY SAIN** had their modest rhyme: "Spahn and Sain and pray for rain." While it is hardly a tribute to the rest of the Boston Braves pitching staff of the late 1940s, it certainly speaks volumes on behalf of Warren and Johnny, pitching cohorts who helped the Braves to the 1948 National League pennant. Sain was a 20-game winner four times in five Boston seasons, while Spahn went on to win 20 or more 13 times on his way to the all-time left-hander's win total of 363, just ten fewer than the league record co-held by those twin mountain peaks known as Mathewson and Alexander.

Sain was known for his assortment of curves large and small, while Spahn threw every pitch in the book. Sore arm? Between 1947 and 1963 Warren never started fewer than 32 games in a season. Spahn and Spahn, on and on.

Pages 176 & 177: It's April 15, 1947, at Brooklyn's Ebbets Field, and one of baseball's most momentous historical events is soon to occur, though you wouldn't have guessed it from the loose, carefree look of the Dodger infield. They are (*left to right*) third baseman **JOHNNY ("SPIDER") JORGENSEN**, shortstop **PEE WEE REESE**, second baseman **EDDIE STANKY**, and the new man, rookie first baseman **JACKIE ROBINSON**. Jackie was the focus. When that game officially got underway, with Robinson in the Dodger lineup, it marked the integration of major league baseball. The acumen of Branch Rickey and the grit of Jackie Robinson were to make the move a success, though it wasn't until 1959 that every major league club had integrated their rosters.

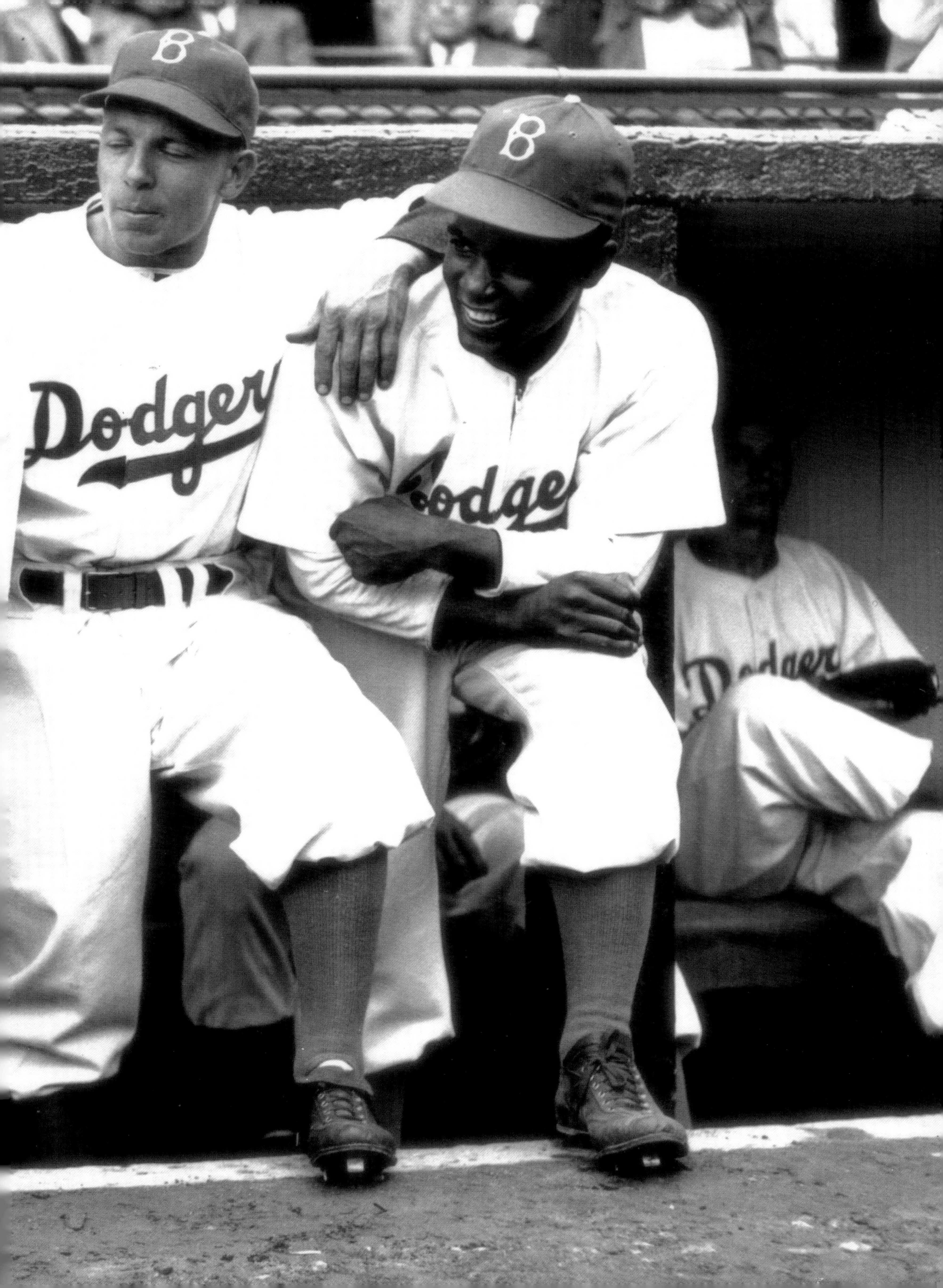
B
B
Dodgers

Index

PHOTOGRAPHY CREDITS

Every attempt has been made to identify the photographers whose work is featured in this volume. Then, as now, photographers in the early part of this century often worked anonymously, selling the rights to their work to newspapers or wire services. While the names of many of these men have been lost to obscurity, we are fortunate to be able to identify the following photographers whose work appears on these pages: